Theos Friends' Progra

Theos is a religion and society think tank which seeks
opinion about the role of faith and belief in society.

We were launched in November 2006 with the supp
Dr Rowan Williams and the Cardinal Archbishop of W
Cardinal Cormac Murphy-O'Connor.

We provide

- high-quality research, reports and publications;
- an events programme;
- news, information and analysis to media companies,
  parliamentarians and other opinion formers.

We can only do this with your help!

Theos Friends receive complimentary copies of all Theos publications, invitations
to selected events and monthly email bulletins.

Theos Associates receive all the benefits of Friends and in addition are invited
to attend an exclusive annual dinner with the Theos Director and team.

If you would like to become a Friend or an Associate, please visit
www.theosthinktank.co.uk or detach or photocopy the form below, and send
it with a cheque to Theos for the relevant amount. Thank you

Yes, I would like to help change public opinion!
I enclose a cheque payable to Theos for: ☐**£60** (Friend) ☐**£300** (Associate)

☐ Please send me information on how to give by standing order/direct debit

Name _____

Address _____

_____ Postcode _____

Email _____

Tel _____

Data Protection Theos will use your personal data to inform you of its activities.
If you prefer not to receive this information please tick here. ☐

*By completing you are consenting to receiving communications by telephone and email.
Theos will not pass on your details to any third party.*

Please return this form to:
Theos | 77 Great Peter Street | London | SW1P 2EZ
S: 97711   D: 36701

Theos – clear thinking on religion and society

Theos is a think tank working in the area of religion, politics and society. We aim to inform debate around questions of faith and secularism and the related subjects of values and identity. We were launched in November 2006, and our first report *'Doing God'; a Future for Faith in the Public Square,* written by Nick Spencer, examined the reasons why faith will play an increasingly significant role in public life.

what Theos stands for

In our post-secular age, interest in spirituality is increasing across Western culture. We believe that it is impossible to understand the modern world without an understanding of religion. We also believe that much of the debate about the role and place of religion has been unnecessarily emotive and ill-informed. We reject the notion of any possible 'neutral' perspective on these issues.

what Theos works on

Theos conducts research, publishes reports, and runs debates, seminars and lectures on the intersection of religion, politics and society in the contemporary world. We also provide regular comment for print and broadcast media. Recent areas of analysis include multiculturalism, Christian education, religious liberty and the future of religious representation in the House of Lords. Future areas of focus will include questions of values in economic policy and practice and the role of religion in international affairs.

what Theos provides

In addition to our independently driven work, Theos provides research, analysis and advice to individuals and organisations across the private, public and not-for-profit sectors. Our unique position within the think tank sector means that we have the capacity to develop proposals that carry values – with an eye to demonstrating what really works.

what Theos believes

Theos was launched with the support of the Archbishop of Canterbury and the Cardinal Archbishop of Westminster, but it is independent of any particular denomination. We are an ecumenical Christian organisation, committed to the belief that religion in general and Christianity in particular has much to offer for the common good of society as a whole. We are committed to the traditional creeds of the Christian faith and draw on social and political thought from a wide range of theological traditions. We also work with many non-Christian and non-religious individuals and organisations.

Religion and Law

Gavin Callaghan

Noel Cox

Frank Cranmer

John Duddington

Conor Gearty

Peter Jones

Jacqueline Laing

Maleiha Malik

David McIlroy

Javier García Oliva

Megan Pearson

Julian Rivers

Russell Sandberg

John Scriven

Charlotte Smith

Nick Spencer (ed)

Roger Trigg

Published by Theos in 2012
© Theos

ISBN 978-0-9562182-8-5

Theos
Licence Department
77 Great Peter Street
London
SW1P 2EZ

T 020 7828 7777
E hello@theosthinktank.co.uk
www.theosthinktank.co.uk

contents

contributors

Gavin Callaghan is a solicitor and a Senior Procurator Fiscal Depute in the Crown Office and Procurator Fiscal Service (Scotland's public prosecution service).

Noel Cox is Head of the Department of Law and Criminology, and Professor of Law at Aberystwyth University.

John Duddington is editor of *Law and Justice*, the Christian Law Review, and is an Associate of the Centre for Law and Religion at Cardiff University.

Conor Gearty is Professor of Human Rights Law at the London School of Economics.

Peter Jones is Emeritus Professor of Political Philosophy at Newcastle University.

Jacqueline Laing is Senior Lecturer in the Department of Law, Governance and International Relations at London Metropolitan University.

Maleiha Malik is Professor of Law at King's College, London, and author of *Discrimination Law: Theory and Practice* (2008) and *Anti-Muslim Prejudice in the West – Past and Present* (2010).

David McIlroy studied law at the Universities of Cambridge and Toulouse and theology at Spurgeon's College. He is a practising barrister, specialising in employment law and banking law.

Javier García Oliva is lecturer in law at Manchester University and a Research Associate at the Centre for Law and Religion at Cardiff University.

Megan Pearson is a doctoral student at the London School of Economics researching the clash between religious freedom and non-discrimination rights.

Julian Rivers is Professor of Jurisprudence at Bristol University and an editor-in-chief of the *Oxford Journal of Law and Religion*.

Russell Sandberg is a lecturer at Cardiff Law School and the author of *Law and Religion* (Cambridge University Press, 2011).

John Scriven is a solicitor working in London and a part time university lecturer. He was Chairman of the Lawyers' Christian Fellowship from 2003 to 2011.

Charlotte Smith is Senior Lecturer in the School of Law at Reading University and Co-Director of the Forum for Legal and Historical Research.

Nick Spencer is the Research Director at Theos.

Roger Trigg is Emeritus Professor of Philosophy at the University of Warwick, and Academic Director of the Centre for the Study of Religion in Public Life, Kellogg College, Oxford.

religion and law: an introduction

Jack Cade's vision of a better future, at least as it is filtered through Shakespeare in Henry VI Part 2, is well known:

> There shall be in England seven halfpenny loaves sold for a penny…all the realm shall be in common…there shall be no money; all shall eat and drink on my score; and I will apparel them all in one livery.

It is not, however, as well known as the response of Dick the Butcher who, overcome with the prospect of such a happy life, knows just how to set about it: "The first thing we do, let's kill all the lawyers." Bankers (and politicians) may have overtaken lawyers in the public's mind as the professions most in need of reform (or eradication) in the never-ending quest for a good society, but Dick's line still never fails to get a laugh.

If lawyers remain a longstanding source of public suspicion, so do the ambitions and loyalties of religious groups. When Shakespeare wrote Henry VI in the early 1590s, the nation was painfully divided over a number of, to us, oddly familiar questions. Could one religious minority be trusted when they apparently owed their ultimate loyalty to a hostile foreign authority? Could another when they clearly wished to reform the state in their own rigid, biblically-literal image, irrespective of what the majority wanted? Could a church really be established over such a religiously diverse people? What business did government have making windows into men's souls in the first place? *Mutatis mutandis*, the questions apply to 2012 just as much as they did in 1591.

There are those who, faced with such seemingly intractable problems, seek to cut the Gordian knot with an easy "religion is a private matter and has no place in public life". With one quick, flashing blade the messy entanglement of religion, freedom, equality, conscience, and justice is done away with, and all are free to get on with living their lives.

Easy, perhaps: but also facile, misleading, unjust, and ultimately oppressive. To imagine that confining the hopes, opinions and behaviour of some people who are defined (usually by others) as "religious" (whatever that means) within the private sphere is in any way a fair or workable solution to the problems of a religiously plural society is to take leave of reality. Those societies that attempted such a solution in the twentieth century were rarely the better for it. No matter how awkward it may be, we are stuck with contested claims of religion within public life – for which we need lawyers or, at least, legal experts.

Sixteen of the best have contributed to this volume. Beyond eschewing the view that religion has no place in public life – an opinion more likely to be found in New Atheist internet chat rooms than serious academic circles – the contributors have little in common other than their legal expertise. Some are religious, some are not, and the beliefs of some remain unknown to the editor. *Religion and Law* has no party line. Contributors were asked to contribute not because they share any particular worldview, whether religious or secular, but because they know whereof they speak.

That was the objective of the volume. In a religious/legal landscape that seems increasingly to be swept with confused alarms of struggle and flight, the intention of *Religion and Law* is to shed a little light. Each of the authors picks up on a key issue of the current debate – although there is invariably overlap, not least when it comes to certain totemic cases – and seeks, in a mere 3,000-4,000 words to inform and educate (and perhaps even entertain) the reader.

In so far as there is a plan to the volume, it is in a movement from the specific to the general, as specific questions of, for example, religious symbols, proportionality, and minority legal orders, give way to broader ones of conscience, belief, human rights, and the moral foundations of law. In reality, this plan is a little misleading, as the more general essays cite cases aplenty just as much as the more specific ones touch on deep and profound questions of principle. Nevertheless, it works as a serviceable thread to lead readers through the volume.

In the opening chapter, Frank Cranmer and Javier García Oliva look at what should, in theory, be a narrow question in the religion and law debate – the question of religious symbols in public life – but one that has become perhaps the biggest and most animated. Why, they ask, are we (meaning not only the British) so much more exercised about this issue than we were fifty years ago? While it is almost a truism to say that every aspect of religion and law could do with more understanding, nowhere is this truer than the question of religious symbols. We need, they suggest, to develop what the philosopher Martha Nussbaum calls "cultivated inner eyes".

Maleiha Malik looks at perhaps the most contentious – or, at least, most misunderstood – area of the debate, 'Minority Legal Orders', often misleadingly called 'parallel legal systems' and synonymous in the public's mind with the question of Islam, Muslims and Sharia law. A cultural or religious group's claim to its own legal system is not necessarily a threat to the state's sovereignty over all its citizens, she argues, but that does not mean that such claims ought automatically to be respected. Malik outlines a number of ways that the state may respond to such a claim, although her fundamental contention is that it must safeguard the rights of those individuals with less power within a Minority Legal Order, such as women, gays and lesbians, who may be at risk of harm. She also argues that, perhaps more than any other in this area, this topic needs more research. We simply do not know enough about people's experience of Minority Legal Orders in Britain to be able to say, with any authority, how we should handle them.

Megan Pearson writes on proportionality, a means of adjudicating human rights claims which aims to ensure that rights are not unnecessarily or overly restricted, without at the same time undermining other important social goods. This approach has much to recommend it to the contentious interface of religion, equality and freedom. It is a structured, clear but flexible method of legal analysis. Most importantly, however, by focusing on fact-specific, relevant, contextual questions, it avoids pronouncing definitively on winners and losers, or escalating individual cases into *casus belli*.

Peter Jones engages with the question of the cost of religious freedom, especially as it arises in cases of indirect religious discrimination. He argues that while freedom of religion or belief rightly means that people have the right to live in accordance with their beliefs, it does not mean that others should necessarily bear the burden of that right. Religious commitment is a serious choice and, as with all serious choices, its implications are not cost free. That does not mean that society should do nothing to mitigate the burdens that people incur when beliefs clash with public or private arrangements; it does, however, mean that when that cost becomes unreasonable, religious believers cannot expect others to pick up the tab.

Russell Sandberg looks at the vexed question of what is belief in the context of "religion and belief", focusing on recent tribunal decisions. He finds more confusion than clarity, not least as the removal of the word "similar" from the original definition – "any religion, religious belief, or similar philosophical belief" – took away the only (if admittedly somewhat crude) means of assessing what constituted 'belief'. Precisely how we should define belief is still far from settled but, Sandberg argues, any workable definition needs to be holistic and to take account of the agency of the believer.

Roger Trigg asks whether there is anything special about religious belief, drawing an instructive comparison of how the issue is dealt with on either side of the Atlantic. 'Religion', he argues, ought to be treated as a distinct case within law, rather than simply being elided with or 'covered' by conscience or speech, still less being dismissed in law as something as irrational or subjective. Failure to do so, he writes, simply results in the kind of unacceptable narrowing and limiting of religious freedom against which America so carefully guards.

Noel Cox examines the media and, in particular, the much-trumpeted right to offend religious believers. He argues that, although we should not impose censorship for fear of offending religious groups, we need to temper our legal rights with a greater awareness of our moral responsibilities. Failure to do so, he contends, constitutes a long-term threat to the theist's freedom of belief.

Gavin Callaghan looks at a religious-legal interface that has been largely ignored, at least until recently: the question of swearing on oath in court. Focusing specifically at Scotland, where the justification of this has recently come under focus, he argues that to remove the ability of Christians to swear in order to accentuate the truthfulness of their evidence would be to deny part of their character, which, paradoxically but importantly, is what is being relied on when giving evidence.

Frank Cranmer gives a spirited defence of the European Court of Human Rights, so often the whipping boy when it comes to questions of religion and law. Much as the media, public and (some) politicians complain about the role that Strasbourg plays within domestic judgments, as a long-established liberal democracy, he argues, the United Kingdom is under a compelling moral obligation to uphold human rights in the wider interests of those elsewhere who are massively less fortunate than ourselves.

John Duddington asks what exactly a conscientious belief is and, if a person holds such a belief, when and in what circumstances this can justify a claim that the law does not and indeed should not apply to them. He notes that a claim to a conscientious belief cannot simply be an assertion of my individual beliefs but must, rather, be based on something deeper. This helps clarify rather than solve the issue of law and conscience, and Duddington concludes by outlining four principles by means of which claims of conscience should be recognised and respected.

Conor Gearty looks at the relationship between (secular) human rights and faith, particularly Roman Catholic faith. He suggests that each partner in this dialogue has something to learn from the other: human rights theory should attend to the Catholic conception of human dignity that is more than just procedural, i.e. a conception which insists that it matters *what* you choose for your life rather than how you choose it; whereas Catholic thought should heed the recognition, in human rights, that to discriminate according to gender and sexuality is to hinder the dignity that Catholic Social Teaching seeks to respect.

John Scriven also looks at human rights, taking a more critical attitude, outlining some of the practical difficulties which spill out from a secular theory of human rights that takes no consideration of commensurate duties. He argues that the current focus on rights, equality and non-discrimination is inadequate to the task, circumventing, as it does, the bigger question of the public good, on which all such debates are founded. By contrast a

Christian concept of the common good, he argues, offers a more compelling framework for addressing issues of conscience.

Jacqueline Laing traces the natural law tradition through the classical and medieval periods and defends it against Bentham's charge that the natural law and therefore also natural rights are "nonsense upon stilts". She argues that it is the idea of the natural law that undergirds human rights with its concern for universal and timeless values. Laing contends that if we want to hold on to the idea that certain activities and actions are timelessly unjust, whether genocide, child abuse, rape, or slavery, then we have to jettison our view that both morality and law in its fullest sense, i.e. that which binds the human conscience, are mere human constructs or social conventions.

Charlotte Smith highlights one of the most ancient and venerable interfaces between religion and law, namely the question of establishment. Reflecting on the English example, she defines establishment or, rather, points out how fluid that definition is, and then outlines the various justifications for its English form. Some of these, she recognises, are no longer tenable but others, in particular the argument that establishment signals that there is a place for religious faith, in all its forms, in public life (increasingly needed in the face of aggressive secularism), remain persuasive – at least for now.

Julian Rivers asks whether English law is Christian and answers with a careful 'yes and no', depending on how one reads the question. If being Christian means directly defending Christianity or promoting the church, the answer, he shows, is no, and has effectively been no for over a century. If, however, it means being consistent with a Christian view of the proper purpose and content of secular law, then it is broadly Christian – although, as Rivers concludes, we cannot assume it will always remain so.

Finally, David McIlroy systematically dismantles the idea that law is a-moral, without foundation in the ethical universe that we all inhabit. We need, instead, he argues, to see it clearly for what it is, a 'branch' or 'sub-category' of morality. This does not mean we should equate law with morality. But because law is a reflection of our substantive, shared moral commitments, we should be more willing to debate, seriously and in a sustained way, what those moral commitments are, and how far they are shared.

"To clarify rather than solve" could serve as an epigraph to *Religion and Law*, and this may frustrate some readers who reach the end of the book with a fateful "And…?" on the tip of their tongue. If so, it is worth noting that this is partly inevitable and partly intentional.

It is inevitable because many of the issues dealt with in this volume are essentially intractable, not amenable to any 'solution', let alone a quick and simple one. Ironically, this in itself constitutes a key reason why religion must be allowed to play a full role in public discourse: because any solution offered will invariably draw on deep beliefs and convictions, concerning (for example) the relative importance of individual freedom, corporate or collective freedom, and public security and order (however they are defined). Maleiha Malik's chapter on Minority Legal Orders rightly argues that empirical research will help us understand and navigate better the issue of legal pluralism. But it will not decide for us what approach government should take to MLOs, any more than it would decide the 'correct' attitude to freedom of conscience, speech, employment, or symbols. Any serious discussion of such issues will invariably draw, in some way, on 'comprehensive doctrines' (whether religious or secular) and to rule out of court those rooted in a religious worldview is fundamentally unjust and unreasonable.

Thus, *Religion and Law*'s inconclusiveness is partly inevitable. But it is also intentional as this is the first of a two volume Theos project on the subject. The second volume, which will appear in 2013, will engage in the same subject but from an explicitly Christian point of view. A single-author project, it will lay out an approach to the issues that have dominated this volume – in particular the appropriate line between religious freedom (however it is expressed) and public justice – that draws, indeed is founded, on Christian principles. This will (self-evidently) not appeal to everyone – including not every contributor to this volume – but it will, nonetheless (it is hoped) be accessible and credible to a wide readership, and offer a more directional approach to the subject.

I would personally like to thank all the contributors to this volume, each of whom has been a pleasure to work with. Academics have (and sometimes deserve) a reputation for obscurantism and an inability to communicate with non-experts. The contributions show that this need not be the case. I would also like to thank the Hinchley Charitable Trust and the Tufton Charitable Trust whose generous donations made both volumes and their dissemination possible.

Theos exists to offer a well-grounded, reasonable, accessible and perhaps even persuasive Christian voice relating to religion in contemporary society. It is my hope that this volume and its successor will do precisely that.

Nick Spencer
Research Director, Theos
September 2012

religious symbols: not just baubles and bangles

introduction

The sight of people wearing overtly-religious clothing and, to a lesser extent, displays of religious insignia, have become increasingly controversial. But it was not always like that.

When the English half of the writing-duo was at grammar school in the late fifties, though none of them sported a skull-cap, all the Jewish boys wore the *tallit katan*, a short, square, blue-and-white undershirt with long tassels (*tzitzit*) at the four corners – and the more keenly-observant left the *tzitzit* hanging out. They did so in response to the biblical injunction to "make them fringes in the borders of their garments…and…put upon the fringe of the borders a ribband of blue."[1] No-one was even remotely upset or offended by this particular religious symbol, even though it was a time when low-level, unconscious anti-Semitism was still fairly rife. It was simply 'what Jewish boys did', along with not attending school prayers and leaving well before sunset on winter Fridays so as to be home in time for *Shabbat*.

Similarly, when the Spanish half of the team attended a state primary school in the early eighties the presence of crucifixes in all the classrooms was completely uncontentious. Perhaps it was just assumed that the Christian-Catholic crucifix, the religious symbol of the overwhelming majority of the pupils, was merely a sign of Spanish and European identity and it simply did not cross anyone's mind that members of other faiths, atheists and agnostics could find it offensive.

So what has changed? The most obvious response is that the last fifty years have seen fairly homogeneous and monocultural societies in Western Europe become multi-ethnic and multi-faith. Muslims and Hindus were small minorities in the United Kingdom in the 1950s. The most recent available figures from the Department of Health suggest that by 2006 there were some 2 million Muslims in Great Britain and some 800,000 Hindus.[2] Secularist France does not, as a matter of principle, collect statistics on racial, ethnic or religious background, but a recent study estimates its Muslim population at some 4.7 million, or 7.5 per cent of the total.[3] But is controversy over religious symbols and religious dress merely a convenient and socially-acceptable vehicle for those who are concerned about immigration and the rise of Islam in the West to vent their racial and religious prejudices while avoiding the charge of outright Islamophobia? Or is it, perhaps, symptomatic of a more general rejection of any kind of 'religion' as an acceptable life-stance? Or is it more complicated even than that?

The refusal to allow a devout Muslim woman member of the Turkish Parliament to wear the *hijab* during debates led to the dispute in *Kavakçi*, in which she argued that she was being denied her right to manifest her religion under Article 9 of the European Convention of Human Rights.[4] In France, *all* 'ostentatious' religious symbols, including Muslim headscarves, Sikh turbans and Jewish skull-caps, were banned from state primary, middle and secondary schools as early as 2004. In April 2011 it became generally illegal to cover one's face in public, which means that a Muslim woman who walks out into the street wearing in a *niqab* veil or a *burqa* now risks a fine of €150 – a state of affairs likely to be challenged in Strasbourg.[5]

By virtue of their Constitutions, though, Turkey and France are strictly secular states – which the United Kingdom is not. Though it may not be an overtly-religious country like, for example, Greece or Malta,[6] neither is it overtly secular. In some ways it stands between the extremes of social secularism and identification with a particular religion: it may still be 'religious' in constitutional terms but its population as a whole is increasingly multi-faith – and with a significant decrease of religious practice overall.

religious dress and recent controversies

Not only are Muslim schoolgirls in Britain not prevented from wearing the hijab, but many Local Education Authorities have also made considerable efforts to negotiate variations from 'standard' school uniform that will satisfy Muslim sensibilities. Similarly, the law accommodates observant Sikhs by exempting their *kirpans* – ritual daggers – from the ban on carrying bladed weapons in public, by allowing them to wear turbans instead of motorcycle crash-helmets, and by excusing Sikhs on construction sites from wearing safety helmets.[7] Equally, if a devout Muslim woman wishes to wear the *hijab* in the House of Commons or the House of Lords no-one is likely to bat an eyelid. But that certainly does not mean that religious dress and the display of religious symbols are simply non-issues for the United Kingdom. Three brief examples will serve to illustrate the problem.

school uniform regulations

There has been a series of disputes about religious dress and school uniform regulations – most, but not all, involving Muslim girls. In *Begum* the House of Lords ruled that Denbigh High School, Luton, was within its rights not to permit Ms Shabina Begum to wear the long *jilbab* coat.[8] At the time of the hearing ten religious groupings were represented at the school – which had a very diverse intake – and almost four-fifths of pupils were Muslim. The school had carried out extensive and detailed consultations with the local Muslim community on the design of its uniform and the House of Lords held that its uniform policy was proportionate and made adequate provision for Muslims. But in doing so it reversed the Court of Appeal's ruling that Ms Begum's rights had indeed been interfered with to an unreasonable degree – which goes to prove how difficult these issues can be.

In *Watkins-Singh*[9] the applicant wished to wear a *kara* bangle at school. Though the *kara* is mandatory for baptised Sikhs as part of the 'Five Ks',[10] Sarikha Watkins-Singh had not yet been baptised. Even so, Mr Justice Silber held that the school's dress code could not forbid the *kara* where the wearer "genuinely believed for reasonable grounds that wearing this item was a matter of exceptional importance to his or her racial identity or his or her religious belief."[11]

Watkins-Singh is a something of a special case because, in an earlier judgment on whether or not a Sikh schoolboy could wear a turban, the House of Lords had held that Sikhs, like Jews, were a racial group for the purposes of the Race Relations Act 1976 – which Christians and Muslims could never be.[12] Nevertheless, it points up very starkly the tensions that can arise between inner conviction and external regulation.

Moreover, school uniform disputes pose a particular conundrum because they almost invariably focus on 'children' which, for legal purposes, means "those under the age of eighteen"; and part of the problem with cases such as *Begum* and *Watkins-Singh* is that judges tend to assume that, *because* they are 'children', school pupils have only a limited capacity to make rational choices for themselves.

It was common ground in *Begum* that Shabina Begum's belief was sincere and no less a religious belief because it might have changed or because it was shared only by a small minority; and Lady Hale further pointed out that adolescents sometimes make moral judgments that differ from those of their parents.[13] Though she did not dissent from the majority, Lady Hale admitted her unease at the proposition that Ms Begum's right to manifest her religion had not been infringed because she had chosen to attend that particular school knowing full well what the school uniform was and had then changed her mind – and that by changing her mind she had somehow forfeited her right to have her views respected.[14] Though the fact that schoolchildren are not yet fully adult might help justify interference with their choices, it was interference nonetheless.[15]

Citing Lady Hale in her support, Maleiha Malik has argued more generally for a 'mature' concept of female autonomy [which] requires a more fluid public space in which different aspects of an individual's culture and religion, as well as their preferences for education and work, can be integrated.[16]

Our only reservation is that, in our view, the principle might equally well be applied to *male* autonomy. Does every Sikh boy keep his hair long out of religious principle or do some give way to parental and peer pressure? Does every Muslim boy about to be circumcised submit willingly to the procedure?

crosses, crucifixes and neck-chains

Chaplin and *Eweida*[17] both involved refusals by employers to allow employees in uniform to wear a cross or crucifix on a neck-chain and, in both cases, the courts held that this had not amounted to religious discrimination because Christians were not obliged to wear them as a necessary part of their observance: rather, it was a matter of personal choice. British Airways' management had said that Nadia Eweida's pendant cross was contrary to their uniform policy; in Shirley Chaplin's case, the Royal Devon and Exeter NHS Trust had explained that the problem was not her crucifix but that front-line staff were prohibited from wearing *any* type of necklace because of health and safety concerns. The complicating factor in Ms Chaplin's case is that she is not, as one might expect, a Roman Catholic but a member of the Free Church of England – a small breakaway Anglican Church that left the mainstream in the 1840s in reaction to Anglo-Catholicism. In coming to its conclusion, the Employment Tribunal consulted her minister, The Revd John Eustice, who was reported in paragraph 17 of the judgment as confirming – unsurprisingly, given his liturgical and theological stance – that members of his Church were not required to wear a crucifix.

At the time of writing the two cases have been conjoined for an appeal at Strasbourg[18] – and the Prime Minister has said in the House of Commons that if the claimants are unsuccessful "we will change the law and make it clear that people can wear religious emblems at work."[19]

religious dress, health and safety and work-wear

In 2007, the Department of Health instituted an obligatory "bare below the elbows" rule for clinical staff in NHS hospitals in England as part of its attempts to control hospital-borne infections. The supporting guidance stated that it was "poor practice…[to] wear hand or wrist jewellery/wristwatch (a plain wedding ring may be acceptable)."[20]

The new rule immediately caused difficulties for observant Muslim women and there were reports that some had objected to wearing short-sleeved medical scrubs or rolling up their sleeves when washing their hands because to do so was immodest.[21] In response, the Department initially proposed separate changing facilities for female Muslim staff, then suggested in revised guidance either sleeves that could be rolled or pulled back during hand-washing and direct patient care or disposable over-sleeves elasticated at elbow and wrist.[22]

How this will develop still remains to be seen. The current 2010 guidance reiterates that "[l]ocal policies may allow a plain ring, such as a wedding ring". To which a baptised Sikh might reasonably retort, "if a plain ring, why not a plain *kara*?" and cite *Watkins-Singh* in support. Moreover, it tends to be forgotten that, though growing secularism has weakened the link, a wedding ring is *itself* a religious symbol, certainly in its origin: "With this ring, I thee wed…"

religious displays in public buildings

Cases about religious symbols are becoming much more frequent in continental European jurisdictions than hitherto. By far the most important has been *Lautsi*,[23] in which a Finnish-born Italian national claimed that the crucifixes on the classroom walls of her children's state school breached the principle of secularism enshrined in the Italian Constitution.

She took the case to Strasbourg and, initially, was successful. The first-instance Court held that the crucifix was of religious as well as of cultural significance and what might be encouraging for some students could be emotionally disturbing for those of other faiths or of none.[24] Therefore, its presence violated the duty of neutrality in providing public services and, specifically Article 2 of Protocol No. 1 (Right to education) taken with Article 9, because it restricted "the right of parents to educate their children in conformity with their convictions and the right of schoolchildren to believe or not believe."

Mancini spoke for many when she welcomed that judgment as a repudiation of what she described as Strasbourg's 'traditional deference' towards domestic approaches to religious freedom and a signal that the rights of religious and ideological minorities were at last being taken seriously.[25] But her hopes were to be dashed when on appeal to the Grand Chamber the earlier decision was overturned by fifteen votes to two.

The Grand Chamber rejected Italy's contention that the issue was simply outside the scope of Article 2 of Protocol No. 1 altogether, but it still concluded that, in principle, the matter was for the Italian Government itself to determine rather than the Court – and in support of that contention pointed to the fact that there was no overall European consensus on the issue. Or as Michael White rather tartly observed in *The Guardian* on the day after the first instance judgment was handed down, "Crucifixes? Italy? Where did Soile Lautsi think she was moving to live? Thailand? What will she campaign to ban next? Pizza, the Mafia, bling, cheating at football?"[26] Which like all good satire contains more than a grain of truth: controversial though its presence may be, in countries such as Italy and Spain the crucifix is as much a cultural as a religious symbol.

Quite apart from the more general human rights point about the relative powers of the European Court of Human Rights and the member Governments of the Council of Europe, *Lautsi* raises the wider issue of the extent to which religious symbols can properly be displayed on secular public buildings generally without giving offence to those of other faiths or none.

The recent decision of Bath and North East Somerset Council to remove a prominent window etched with a cross and replace it with plain glass as part of its refurbishment of Haycombe Crematorium is a case in point. The decision triggered a petition from those who claimed that the crematorium was a 'chapel' and that the window should either be left as it was or replaced with another cross – and evoked an equally strong reaction in favour of the proposal from those who felt that an overtly-Christian symbol had no place in a building used by people of all faiths and none. Many local authorities, however, have quietly removed fixed religious insignia from their crematoria and instead provide portable items such as a cross, a crucifix or a *Magen David* that can be used as needed to accommodate the particular religious sensibilities of the mourners.

conclusion

Why have religious dress and the public display of religious symbols assumed such a high profile in recent years? Is it simply a side-effect of increased religious diversity and the fact that overtly-religious costume is seen much more often in public that was the case twenty or thirty years ago? Could it be, perhaps, that people who might in earlier times have regarded themselves in some sense as 'default' or 'cultural' Christians have now come down on the side of humanism and tend to support the secularist agenda? Might it be that the Human Rights Act 1998 has raised awareness of 'human rights' and made people more willing to assert those rights? Is it because, as religious practice becomes less a matter of social conformity and more of personal affirmation, those who are observant are tending to be more tenacious about their observance than their parents were? Or is it a combination of all these factors to some degree?

In a recent discussion of religious symbols in schools, McClean poses an interesting question: why should it be a socio-legal issue for a Muslim woman to wear a headscarf but not for an Englishman to wear a Manchester United shirt?[27] In so saying, he goes to the heart of the matter of 'religious' – or perhaps tribal – dress in an increasingly secular society, not least because of the degree of low-level public disorder that has traditionally surrounded association football matches.

"Baubles, bangles and beads" sang the heroine in the 1950s musical *Kismet*; and that just about sums up the attitude of many critics to issues of religious dress and the display of religious symbols. If only religious people would grow up and get a grip, suggest secularists and humanists, they could stop fretting over silly superstitions about crosses, crucifixes, bangles, headscarves and suchlike and start behaving like rational human beings.

But not only is that attitude intensely patronising – a *kara* is not costume jewellery and nor, for Shirley Chaplin, is a crucifix – it is also based on a totally unrealistic view of what makes people tick. However irrational faith may appear to the secularist, for believers it is a fundamental element both of self-understanding and of the way in which they relate to others – and, if recent experience is any guide, there are no signs that religion is about to wither away in the foreseeable future.

In an oral comment at a recent workshop on schools and religious freedom at University College, London, Maleiha Malik suggested that "for an observant Muslim girl that extra eighteen inches of material can be desperately important".[28] But why should some people find that extra eighteen inches of material quite so worrying? McClean's rather disturbing reply to his own question may give us some clue:

> [W]e associate Buddhism with safely abstract meditation; we find Hinduism colourful and cheerful, we treat Jewish practice with an embarrassed awareness of…anti-Semitism…; but we fear Islam as a threat to our security and the Christian faith.[29]

There seems to have been a fundamental shift in religious perceptions over the past few decades. In the eyes of its critics, 'religion' can only be tolerated so long as it is cosy and anodyne, which is why religious symbols in general and Islamic religious dress in particular have become so controversial. What appears to be lacking is what Martha Nussbaum calls "cultivated inner eyes" – the ability to stand in the shoes of the other person:

> The idea that equal respect requires us to approve of all religions equally, or even all instances of religious conduct, is just mistaken, and the participatory imagination doesn't require approval either. It just requires seeing the other as a person pursuing human goals, and understanding in some loose way what those goals are, so that one can see what a burden to their conscience it is, and whether the conduct really does contravene vital state interests.[30]

So, as we implied in our introduction, might the whole issue of religious symbols merely be a displacement activity for hidden or unacknowledged racism or xenophobia? Clearly, there must be a good deal more to it than that – but we suspect that McClean's comment contains considerably more than a grain of truth. He firmly rejects the notion that there should be some new legal provision under which people would be able to avoid being exposed to religious symbols, which he describes as "the odd notion of a negative right, not to face religion".[31] And so do we: social cohesion in a multi-faith society requires a considerable degree of "live and let live" – and hang-ups about *hijabs* do not help that process.

references

1   Numbers 15.38 (*Authorised Version*).

2   B. Burford et al, *Religion or belief: a practical guide for the NHS* (London: Central Office of Information, 2009). The estimates do not include Northern Ireland.

3   Its estimate for the current Muslim population of the UK as a whole is 2.8 million: see Forum on Religion and Public Life, *The Future of the Global Muslim Population* (Washington DC: Pew Research Center, January 2011) pp. 126–7.

4   *Kavakçi v Turkey* [2007] 71907/01 ECHR. In the end, her political party was dissolved altogether; and the ECtHR held that because that had contravened Article 3 of Protocol No. 1 (free elections) it was not necessary to consider whether her right to manifest her religion had also been violated.

5   See Angelique Christafis, 'France's *burqa* ban: women are "effectively under house arrest"', *The Guardian* (19 September 2011) http://www.guardian.co.uk/world/2011/sep/19/battle-for-the-burqa Accessed 8 July 2012. The prohibition does not apply to face-coverings "required or permitted by the provisions of statute or regulations" or for health and safety reasons – presumably such items as crash-helmets and welders' masks – or which are worn for "sporting, festive or artistic or traditional displays".

6   Article 3 of the Greek Constitution declares that "The prevailing religion...is that of the Eastern Orthodox Church of Christ". Article 2 of the Maltese Constitution declares that "The religion of Malta is the Roman Catholic Apostolic Religion" and that "The authorities of the Roman Catholic Apostolic Church have the duty and the right to teach which principles are right and which are wrong".

7   Criminal Justice Act 1988 s 139(5)(b) and Carrying of Knives etc. (Scotland) Act 1993 s 1(5); Road Traffic Act 1988 s16, (which re-enacted the terms of the Motor-Cycle Helmets (Religious Exemption) Act 1976); Employment Act 1989 s11.

8   *R (on the application of Begum) v Headteacher and Governors of Denbigh High School* [2006] UKHL 15.

9   *R (on the application of Watkins-Singh) v The Governing Body of Aberdare Girls' High School* [2008] EWHC (Admin) 1865.

10 *Kesh* (uncut hair), the *kangha* (a wooden comb), the *kara* (a metal bracelet), the *kachera* (cotton undershorts tied with a drawstring) and the *kirpan*.

11 *Watkins-Singh*, op. cit., at para 56.

12 *Mandla v Dowell Lee* [1982] UKHL 7.

13 *Begum*, op. cit., at para 21.

14 Ibid., at para 92.

15 Ibid., at para 93.

16 Maleiha Malik, 'Progressive Multiculturalism: Minority Women and Cultural Diversity' *International Journal on Minority and Group Rights* 17/3 (2010) pp. 447-467.

17   *Chaplin v Royal Devon and Exeter Hospital NHS Foundation Trust* [2010] ET 1702886/2009, *Eweida v British Airways Plc* [2010] EWCA Civ 80.

18   See *Nadia Eweida and Shirley Chaplin v United Kingdom* [2011] 48420/10 ECHR 738

19   Hansard, HC (Series 5) vol. 544, col 306 (11 July 2012).

20   *Uniforms and Workwear: an evidence base for developing local policy* (London: Department of Health 2007) p. 9. See also 'New NHS uniform' (Scottish Government News Release, 16 December 2008).

21   See, for example, Julie Henry and Laura Donnelly, 'Female Muslim medics "disobey hygiene rules"': *Daily Telegraph* (4 February 2008). The rule would also, in principle, ban the *kara*.

22   *Uniforms and Workwear: Guidance on uniform and workwear policies for NHS* employers (London: Department of Health, 26 March 2010).

23   *Lautsi & Ors v Italy* [2011] 30814/06 ECHR (GC).

24   *Lautsi v Italy* [2009] 30814/06 ECHR.

25   Susanna Mancini 'La Supervisione Europea presa sulserio: la Controversia sul Crocifissotra Margine di Apprezzamento e Ruolo contro-maggioriario della Corte', *Corso di Pubblicazione su 'Giurisprudenza Costituzionale'* (2009) Fascicolo n. 5 p. 10.

26   Michael White, 'Italy's crucifix case and UK's climate change decision: for God's sake leave religion out of this', *The Guardian* (4 November 2009) www.guardian.co.uk/politics/blog/2009/nov/04/italy-crucifix-climate-change-cgod Accessed 8 July 2012.

27   David McClean, 'Religious Dress and Symbols in Schools', in Gerhard Robbers (ed.) *Religion In Public Education / La Religion Dans L'Éducation Publique* (European Consortium for Church and State Research: Trier, 2011) p. 27.

28   Quoted with permission.

29   McClean, 'Religious Dress', op. cit., p. 27.

30   Martha C. Nussbaum, *The New Religious Intolerance* (Cambridge, MA: Harvard University Press, 2012) p. 143.

31   McClean, 'Religious Dress', op. cit., p. 27.

religious minorities and law: understanding minority legal orders in the UK

Religious law and religious courts have become a controversial topic in recent years. Archbishop Rowan Williams' statement in February 2008 that some religious communities, such as British Muslims, could share jurisdiction with state law has been a catalyst for subsequent public debates. The statement was followed by public denunciations of Islamic (sharia) law and "decontextualisation, exaggeration and misinformation".[1]

Since 9/11 and 7/7, public debate about religious law in the UK has focused on Islamic law (sharia). Muslims have often been presented as an aggressive threat to liberal democracies. It has been assumed that British Muslims want unilaterally to impose their values on the majority population. This assumption is encouraged by the popular association of sharia with cruel criminal punishments, such as the stoning of women or the amputation of limbs, which are sometimes implemented by some foreign countries that have a Muslim majority.[2] Although these extreme examples relate to foreign countries, the international context continues to have a considerable influence on the domestic debate.

British Muslims are closely associated with religious law. They are also religious minorities who are at risk of prejudice because of their attachment to religious law, and the public perception that they are separating themselves from mainstream institutions to follow their own legal system. In the past, a recurrent stereotype about Jews was that their attachment to the Old Testament and their religious law was evidence of 'barbaric' customs surrounding diet, slaughter of animals and the treatment of women.[3] Similar processes can be observed in the context of Muslim minorities, especially after 9/11 and 7/7. In public debates and in the media, British Muslims are often presented as a threatening and 'barbaric' social group because of their religious attachment to Islamic legal norms in ways that foster fear, hatred and prejudice.[4]

Since 9/11 and 7/7, Islamic law has become a focus for political extremism by Muslims and non-Muslims. A vicious cycle has emerged in which Muslim extremist groups such as Islam4UK and Al Muhajiroun demand implementation of sharia and an 'Islamic state', thereby adding fuel to the prevailing discourse of racist far right groups that object to 'Islamic law in the UK' and the 'Islamisation of Britain'. There is no evidence that groups such as Islam4UK or Al Muhajiroun have any substantial following within the Muslim community.[5] Yet, in media discourses and the popular imagination it is often misleadingly assumed that significant numbers of British Muslims are seeking the wholesale import of a foreign legal system that requires amputation of limbs or the stoning of women, and which will be imposed on all British citizens.[6]

The framing of the contemporary debate as a problem of stoning or the amputation of limbs not only encourages prejudice and hatred of British Muslims, and distorts an analysis of the claims of British Muslims,[7] but it also has detrimental consequences for other cultural and religious minorities, even if they are not the ultimate target of concerns, anxieties or legal regulation. A reasonable public debate has not been possible. In this context, religious law and religious courts have been misleadingly presented as 'parallel legal systems' that are an ominous threat to liberal democracies. The term 'parallel legal systems' is inaccurate and misleading. This is because religious law and religious courts do not exist in a 'parallel' social world that is unrelated to state law or the lives of mainstream populations. 'Minority Legal Order (MLO)', rather than 'parallel legal system', is a more accurate description of the religious legal norms or the religious courts and institutions that are present in the UK. Minority Legal Orders raise questions about a wide range of issues that should be debated because they are of critical importance, not only for minorities but also for all citizens within increasingly diverse liberal democracies.

In the UK, there are religious institutions that interpret, apply and enforce some aspects of religious law. Courts of the Church of England are treated as part of the state legal system. Jews, Muslims and Catholics have established religious councils that deal with civil disputes but these are not recognised by state law. Any person who commits a criminal offence is liable to be prosecuted for that offence when it is in the public interests to do so, irrespective of the norms of religious law or the decision of a religious council. In some civil matters, individual members of religious communities have the option of voluntarily following the decisions of their own community institutions. These decisions are subject to state law and they cannot be automatically enforced through the state legal system.

This chapter is a selective rather than a comprehensive analysis of minority legal orders. Its aim is to open up, re-frame and encourage not only academic and policy research but also public debate about minority legal orders in liberal democracies. A more detailed analysis is set out in the full British Academy Policy Centre report *Minority Legal Orders in the UK: Minorities, Pluralism and the Law*.[8]

what is a minority legal order?

There are a number of features of communal cultural and religious life in the UK that make it appropriate to speak about minority legal orders (MLOs). First, we can say that a community has an MLO when its way of life includes some aspects of the characteristics we often associate with law and legal order. An MLO can be defined around two aspects: first, by its distinct cultural or religious norms; second, by some 'systemic' features that allow us to say that there is a distinct institutional system for the identification, interpretation and enforcement of these norms. Whether or not a community has an MLO may be a matter of degree rather than a clear-cut issue.

The assumption that a cultural or religious community may have law or a legal order raises fear and anxiety. Yet, this fear is misplaced because law and legal order in this context are associated with minority relations with the majority or with state power. Therefore, in terms of political power, the state is the sovereign legal system. Other forms of normative social regulation (promoting particular common values or standards of behaviour) that exercise authority over the lives of individuals are 'subordinate' or a 'minority legal order', and are subject to regulation by the state legal system.

Nevertheless, there may be some situations where the minority legal order commands greater legitimacy and authority within the minority community than state law. The MLO may have a large number of diverse traditions; however, this internal plurality may be hidden to those outside the MLO, when those with the most power within the MLO back one solution which is then presented as the one and only governing norm that is authentic and legitimate. MLOs in the UK mainly accept the supremacy of the state system. There is also a high degree of interaction between MLOs and the state system. So, it may be more accurate to describe an MLO as a 'subordinate' legal order.

'Law' used in the context of religious law is a cause for considerable controversy and confusion. In some situations, the state legal system may recognise or incorporate the MLO's norms, with the consequence that these norms become law in the ordinary sense because they become part of the official state legal system. On the other hand, some individuals or groups such as Jews and Muslims may refer to themselves as having distinct 'law' or a 'legal tradition'. This self-understanding, however, may be a very different concept of 'law' as compared with state law.

For some minority groups, 'law' is a term that refers to a 'folk concept': that is, it refers to norms that permit guidance and regulation of individual and community conduct. Different cultural communities, and especially religious communities, may have a different perception of what is meant by 'law' within their own traditions. In some situations, there may be no necessary tension or conflict between their understanding of themselves as having 'law' and the state's claim that the national legal system is 'sovereign'.

Moreover, the claim by a cultural group that they have 'law' or a 'legal system' does not have to be, necessarily, seen as a threat to the state's sovereignty over all its citizens. In many situations, the cultural group's claim to have 'law' or a 'legal system' will not be an ideological claim to political or legal power. Many of these cultural or religious groups do not seek to compete with the state, or to control public policy or social arrangements for the whole political community. In most cases, the claims of 'law' or 'legal system' by minority cultural or religious groups are strictly limited to a concern with their own group members, usually seeking to define and perpetuate their cultural, religious or ethical custom over a period of time. For instance, the group may seek to define how to create or dissolve families within their community rather than imposing these norms on all citizens. This focus on perpetuation and preservation of culture does, however, raise an issue about the control over the individuals within these communities. Where these cultural or religious customs cause harm to individuals within the group, it may be justified for the state to intervene in order to safeguard individual constitutional or human rights.

minority legal orders in a liberal democracy

Membership of groups in liberal democracies is becoming more complex. There is fluidity and hybridity of cultural exchange, with constant movement of individuals between different cultural and religious communities as well as different social spheres.

It is increasingly accepted that individuals have choices about their identity and group membership, but the reality is that groups can exercise considerable power over their individual members. Special attention needs to be paid to the right to exit, to ensure that individuals do not come within the control of a minority legal order without their consent. There are also more complex situations where individuals want to remain members of a minority group, but they also want to renegotiate the terms of that membership.

Some 'minorities within minorities' such as women, the young and elderly, gays and lesbians, will require special attention because they may face particular pressure to comply with norms within their social group, but lack the power to secure their best interests. Women may need special attention: minority legal orders often focus on family law precisely because these norms control women and enable the preservation of group identity through childrearing. The liberal state is under an obligation to act to protect vulnerable persons, such as women within certain minorities, from harm. A focus on threshold criteria such as 'significant harm' provides a universal guide to state regulation of a minority legal order irrespective of ethnic, cultural or religious difference.

possible UK state responses to minority legal orders

A liberal state faced with a minority legal order can choose one or a combination of the following approaches, which will often overlap:

(1) Prohibition of a minority legal order. This may not be a valid option for several reasons: out of principle, because the MLO may be important for the individual's exercise of autonomy. It also may not be practical. The state system may not have the power to ensure compliance and the MLO may continue to defy the state despite prohibition.

(2) Non-interference with a minority legal order. This may be problematic where the MLO causes significant harm that justifies regulation by the state. A right to exit will often not be a sufficient guarantee that the rights of individuals within minority legal orders, especially the more vulnerable such as women, gays and lesbians, are protected.

(3) Recognition of the minority legal order through granting minority group rights or establishing a personal law system. This has the disadvantage of entrenching the MLO as an 'identity marker' that is resistant to dynamic cultural change. It makes it more difficult for individuals to move between different cultural and religious communities and social spheres.

(4) Cultural Voluntarism. This allows the minority legal order to function but maintains the right of state law to pick and choose whether, and how, it wants to recognise and accommodate the MLO, when enforcing its own liberal norms. The state can use the principle of severance to decide which substantive issues conform to state 'liberal' public policy and which do not. Severance involves the separation of the different norms and rules of behaviour that are contained within a minority legal order so that each can be assessed and evaluated independently of the whole system.

(5) Mainstreaming goes one step further than Cultural Voluntarism. It actively endorses, incorporates or adopts the social norm of the minority legal order within the state legal system, and is based on the assumption that the norm does not conflict with fundamental constitutional principles. This could be done through techniques such as widening existing legal concepts, designing legislative solutions or granting an exemption.

Mainstreaming can be successful where it is the result of active cooperation between the state and the minority legal order to solve a particular problem. For example, The Divorce (Religious Marriages) Act 2002 has assisted in providing a solution for those Jewish women who are unable to gain a divorce where their husbands do not give consent.

The disadvantage of mainstreaming is that minorities would have to convince the state system or a majority of their co-citizens that their cultural or religious practice should be accommodated. This can be difficult if minorities lack political power and are not able to participate in democratic processes. The advantage is that majorities would feel that they have been part of any process to grant recognition or accommodation, giving the MLO greater credibility in the eyes of all citizens.

concluding comments

We know that minority legal orders are already operating in the UK, but future academic research is required to identify which communities, other than Christians, Jews and Muslims, can be said to have MLOs. Academic research also needs to focus on: the experience and impact of MLOs on women users; the impact of state policies on the procedures and substantive rules of the MLO; and ways in which MLOs may offer principles or procedures that have some perceived advantages over the state system.

A move towards greater recognition of MLOs may have some advantages, such as promoting autonomy for minorities, or a greater coalescence between the experiences of individuals in their private lives and their experience of normative political and legal institutions. Significantly, the Arts and Humanities Research Council's research on Social Cohesion and Civil Law confirmed that the religious tribunals that it studied "provide an important service for those Jews, Muslims and Christians for whom a religious divorce 'in the sight of God' is important from both a spiritual and religious legal perspective".[9] None of the three tribunals examined had legal status or were seeking state recognition. Their authority derived from their religious status and it extended only to those who chose to submit to those institutions.

Nevertheless, there will still be a need for safeguards to protect vulnerable individuals who voluntarily participate in the minority legal order but who may suffer harm. Statutory bodies such as the Equality and Human Rights Commission are ideally placed to examine the impact of minority legal orders on users such as women. They are also well placed to develop a system for regulatory oversight to support users, such as women seeking a religious divorce, who want to challenge the procedures or decisions of a minority legal order.

Future policy research could focus on identifying areas of cooperation between the state system and the MLO; for instance, devising solutions for greater recognition of religious marriages and religious divorce within the mainstream system that obviates the need for women to use the MLO. Although there are good reasons to encourage cooperation between the state and minority legal orders, research needs to consider the impact of the current extreme financial pressures on public funding for access to justice. For instance, mediation services run by untrained mediators might fail to accommodate the distinct needs of users from minority groups. Or financial constraints may motivate the state to offer mediation services by untrained mediators within a minority legal order as a 'cheaper' option for some minority communities.

In practice, the financial pressures on legal aid funding and the capacity of the EHRC may mean that vulnerable individual users of the minority legal order are left with no redress in those situations where they have been victims of injustice: for instance, when they want to resile from an enforceable but unfair arbitration agreement, or when they have been subjected to unjust group norms that they later want to renegotiate or challenge. Lack of access to mainstream legal justice or the failure of the mainstream state legal system to accommodate minorities may drive users towards minority legal orders without the protections available within state law.

At present, there are considerable empirical gaps in our understanding of the way in which the substantial norms are being adapted, interpreted and applied in minority legal orders. We know very little about the experience of users of MLOs. Crucially, we do not have enough information to evaluate whether an MLO is entrenching unjust outcomes or whether it is securing autonomy for individual users. Crucially, any state response must safeguard the rights of women, gays and lesbians who are caused harm by the minority legal order. Further research is necessary to allow the design of appropriate law and social policy by the state, non-state actors and MLOs. This body of knowledge can also provide the basis for future public debates about minority legal orders in the UK.

This paper is adapted from the author's report for the British Academy Policy Centre Minority legal orders in the UK: Minorities, pluralism and the law *(2012).*

Copies of the report are available at http://www.britac.ac.uk/policy/Minority-legal-orders.cfm

The author is grateful to all who contributed to the development of that report, including the British Academy Steering Group, peer reviewers, and all who advised the steering group and helped scope the subject area, remotely and in person, as well as attendees of a forum held to discuss a first draft in September 2011.

The British Academy, established by Royal Charter in 1902, champions and supports the humanities and social sciences across the UK and internationally. As a Fellowship of 900 UK humanities scholars and social scientists, elected for their distinction in research, the Academy is an independent and self-governing organisation, in receipt of public funding. Its Policy Centre, which draws on funding from ESRC and AHRC, oversees a programme of activity, engaging the expertise within the humanities and social sciences to shed light on policy issues, and commissioning experts to draw up reports to help improve understanding of issues of topical concern. This report has been peer reviewed to ensure its academic quality. Views expressed in it are those of the author and are not necessarily endorsed by the British Academy but are commended as contributing to public debate.

references

1   Kerry Moore, Paul Mason and Justin Lewis, *Images of Islam in the UK: The Representation of British Muslims in the National Print News Media 2000-2008* (Cardiff School of Journalism, Media and Cultural Studies, 2008), p. 32.

2   Ibid., pp. 32-34.

3   Didi Herman, *An Unfortunate Coincidence: Jews, Jewishness and English Law* (Oxford: Oxford University Press, 2011).

4   Moore, Mason and Lewis, op. cit., pp. 32-34; See also Nicholas Bamforth, Maleiha Malik and Colm O'Cinneide, *Discrimination Law: Theory and Context* (London: Sweet and Maxwell, 2008), chapter 12.

5   Muslim leaders at one of Birmingham's largest mosques supported the Home Secretary's ban on Islam4UK and its parent organisation Al-Muhajiroun, which both call for the establishment of an Islamic state and the implementation of sharia law. See 'Muslim Leaders support the Home Secretary's ban on Islam4UK', *Birmingham Mail* (16 January 2010).

6   Maulana Shahid Raza (Chair of the Mosques and Imams National Advisory Body), a leading Muslim scholar, stated that 'We are not asking for the introduction or the acceptance of Islamic criminal law in this country'. See A. ul Hoque, and P. Shah, *Religare: UK Report on Fieldwork* 25-26, December 2011 (copy on file with the author).

7   Moore, Mason and Lewis concluded, "We found journalists' discussion of Sharia law in Britain regularly and consistently focused on violence, barbarism and irrationality. In 52% of stories, we found the dominant frame to be either concerned with Islamic threat to British culture, the delegitimation of Williams, or the construction of Islam as violent. [...] In our analysis of the acts that newspapers associated with Sharia Law, we found that the three most frequent were stoning (26%), limbs/limb removal (16%) and beheading/execution (11%) [...] This emphasis on brutality was underpinned visually in news reports, which depicted stoning, flogging and beheading in Iran and Afghanistan." (Moore, Mason and Lewis, op. cit., pp. 32-33).

8   A copy of the full report can be downloaded at http://www.britac.ac.uk/policy/Minority-legal-orders.cfm

9   G. Douglas, N. Doe, S. Gilliat-Ray, R. Sandberg, and A. Khan, *AHRC Social Cohesion and Civil Law: Marriage, Divorce and Religious Courts* (Cardiff: Cardiff University, 2011), p. 48.

proportionality: a way forward for resolving religious claims?

introduction

It is hardly revelatory to say that using a sledgehammer to crack a nut is neither efficient nor rational. In a basic sense, then, proportionality is easy to understand and to approve. We expect this general idea of proportionality to be reflected in our legal system: we expect the 'punishment to fit the crime' in sentencing and hope that laws react proportionally to the problems they seek to rectify.

Although the basic idea of proportionality is an ancient one, it has also developed into a strict legal concept used to assess the legality or constitutionality of laws and government action. The purpose of this essay is to demonstrate that proportionality in this sense, taken seriously, provides a coherent and advantageous method for deciding contentious issues relating to religious freedom.

Proportionality as a method of controlling government action originated in nineteenth century Prussian administrative law.[1] It became particularly important in Germany's post-war jurisprudence interpreting the Basic Law (Germany's constitution), although it is not explicitly mentioned in the document. From these beginnings, it has spread widely, being used in national legal systems, such as South Africa, New Zealand, Canada and Israel, and also in the supranational systems of the European Union and European Convention on Human Rights (ECHR). It has also received support in British cases where Convention rights are an issue, including areas such as housing and immigration.[2]

structure of proportionality

Proportionality is a method of adjudicating rights claims. It aims to ensure that rights are not unnecessarily or overly restricted, but not at the expense of undermining important social goals. At its heart is a balancing test: when the benefits of a measure are weighed against the interference with a right, is the interference proportionate to the benefits? It might reduce crime to install CCTV in every home but given the extreme loss of privacy this would involve this policy cannot be proportionate. Proportionality, though, is more sophisticated than a simple balancing of pros and cons.

More precisely, the test is made up of four stages. Each stage should be taken sequentially and must be passed. The four stages are:

(1) Legitimate aim

The reason for restricting a right must be a proper one in a liberal democratic society. Examples might be to increase public safety or to preserve the rights of others. In the CCTV example given above there could be a legitimate aim of reducing crime. If the purpose were to monitor political opposition to the government this would not be legitimate: this is not acceptable in a democratic society.

(2) Rational Connection between Aim and Measure

The measure must actually be capable of promoting the aim. Continuing the example, it is rational to think that installing CCTV cameras would reduce crime within the home and would therefore pass this test. It does not mean that the government must prove that the policy will *definitely* promote the aim. Governments could ban tobacco advertising with the aim of reducing smoking, even though they could not absolutely prove that smoking would thereby be reduced.

Normally this test is easy to pass – governments do not tend to act completely irrationally. However, a Canadian case did fail this test.[3] Immigration rules meant that a child of a Canadian father born outside Canada could obtain citizenship automatically if the birth had been registered with the Canadian authorities. A child of a Canadian mother had to go through a far more complex procedure which included criminal record and security checks. The legitimate aim given for the policy was protecting the safety of Canadian citizens. However, this aim did not bear a rational connection to the discriminatory policy: there was simply no reason to assume that the child of a Canadian mother would be more dangerous than the child of a Canadian father.

(3) No less restrictive means

This is sometimes also called the 'necessity' test. A measure is 'necessary' if there are no less restrictive means of fulfilling the goal *to the same extent*. It is not sufficient if another measure would interfere with the right less but not equally fulfil the conflicting purpose. To take the CCTV example again, a policy that required CCTV only where the person had previous convictions for criminal acts taking place within the home would be less restrictive of the right to privacy, but would not pursue the aim of crime prevention to the same extent. The policy would therefore pass this stage.

(4) Balancing

This is often the most important part of proportionality. It requires the extent and seriousness of the infringement of the right to be weighed against the importance of the conflicting interest and prohibits measures that impose a disproportionate impact. It would be at this stage that CCTV policy would be ruled impermissible.

advantages of proportionality

Proportionality thus provides a structured, clear, but flexible method of analysis. It also inherently requires deliberation and justification, permitting both sides an opportunity to put forward their arguments based on the facts as they particularly apply to them. It demands that those who seek to restrict a right are able to provide sufficient and suitable justification to those whom these acts affect. Rights are often restricted unnecessarily not because of any malice but because a policy's impact in a particular case has not been considered or because those making decisions over-estimate the importance to society of their own goals simply because they are focused on them. Proportionality guards against these dangers.

Proportionality also has specific advantages for questions relating to religious claims. These lie in the nature of the questions it asks. Many cases in this area have become part of a narrative of 'persecution' or an 'anti-Christian agenda', or, alternatively, evidence that religionists are intent on bringing about a kind of theocracy. Cases, which are often about fairly small, albeit important, issues to the parties, become symbols for an entire cultural disagreement. Religion may be a "conversation stopper",[4] but it is often an argument starter.

A proportionality analysis seeks to sidestep such arguments. It makes no attempt to answer all moral and political questions. It merely asks whether the increased (and only the increased) benefit created by a particular measure is sufficient compared to the interference caused by the measure. For example, if a policy interfered with the right of non-discrimination in order to increase religious freedom, the question would not be whether non-discrimination generally was more important than religious freedom. Rather it would ask: is the 'amount' of loss of freedom from discrimination that is generated by this policy, proportionate to the 'amount' of religious freedom generated? By asking a fact-specific contextual question it can cut through the morass of claims and counter-claims. Since judgments only provide a context-specific answer they do not make one side a winner and another a loser permanently.[5] Proportionality can thereby resolve matters without artificially ending debate on issues on which there is no agreement. It is, therefore, ideal for circumstances where there is serious moral disagreement.

David Beatty, a leading academic proponent of proportionality, refers to an Israeli Supreme Court case, *Horev v Minister of Transportation*,[6] as an example of how proportionality could possibly be used to lower tensions.[7] The case concerned whether traffic could be banned in an ultra-Orthodox street in Jerusalem on the Sabbath. Justice Barak, the President of the Court, used an extremely fact-specific proportionality analysis to resolve the case. He argued that if the street were closed all that would be required from non-religious residents was a two-minute detour, which could be balanced against the right of the religious residents to tranquillity during prayer time (he did not permit closure for the whole of the Sabbath as the religious residents had demanded). It is, therefore, possible that, although the situation remained complex, "the judicial inquiry thus turned a dispute that was viewed as a bitter cultural war and a matter of fundamental principle into a simple trade off that most reasonable people would accept."[8]

proportionality and religious freedom

As mentioned above, the advantages of proportionality have been recognised in principle by British courts and a proportionality-type test is used in deciding whether there is justification for indirect employment discrimination.[9] Its strict use, though, in the religious freedom context is fairly rare. Proportionality was used in one of the first cases about the extent of Article 9 of the ECHR. This case, *Williamson*, concerned a religiously-based belief in the need for corporal punishment in private Christian schools.[10] Once it had been decided that such a belief was sufficient for the purposes of Article 9, the House of Lords went on to consider whether there was sufficient justification for the law, basing their decision on proportionality. This led to the unsurprising conclusion that a prohibition on corporal punishment in schools was justified because of the rights of the children. This is a clear example of a straightforward proportionality analysis.

In other cases, though, proportionality is either not used, or is used in such a restrictive way that it becomes meaningless. An example of this is *Eweida v British Airways Plc*.[11] The case concerned a member of British Airways' check-in staff who was forbidden from wearing a cross over her uniform. Instead of focusing on the need for the policy, the case revolved around the very different question of the technical concept of indirect religious discrimination and, in particular, whether she could demonstrate group disadvantage. This required proof that there were others who shared her belief, a difficult matter in such cases where belief can be highly personal and idiosyncratic.

In addition to the discrimination claim, Eweida claimed a violation of Article 9, which should have required a proportionality test if an interference with her right could be established. However, the Court of Appeal merely responded by quoting the European Court of Human

Rights (ECtHR) in saying that "Article 9 does not protect every act motivated or inspired by a religion or belief. Moreover, in exercising his freedom to manifest his religion, an individual may need to take his specific situation into account."[12] All of this is unassailable, but it does not answer *which* acts are protected or *why* this act is not protected.

Of course, even under the most generous test, Eweida would still have to show that she was manifesting her belief – but on the facts as described in the judgment there are at least grounds from which this conclusion can be drawn. Evidently a cross is a Christian symbol and she seemed to suggest that wearing a visible cross was part of her commitment to demonstrate and share her faith, even though it is not a religiously-mandated practice.

This is not the end of the matter: proportionality does not require all religious practices to be protected. However, it seems likely that Eweida would have won her case if proportionality had been considered more strictly. Such an approach could run as follows:

(1) British Airways has a legitimate aim of maintaining 'brand uniformity'.

(2) There is a rational connection between preventing Eweida wearing a cross and this aim.

(3) There is no less restrictive means of achieving this aim than refusing to let her wear a cross given that she wished to wear it visibly in a customer facing job.

(4) The case, therefore, comes down to whether British Airways' interest in maintaining its uniform policy is suitable justification for infringing the right to manifest a belief. To this the answer seems to be no. The maintenance of brand identity, although important, could not be of overriding significance to BA because it permitted exceptions for other religious clothing and it had, in fact, abandoned the policy in the face of significant public criticism by the time of the hearing. Furthermore, a small cross is hardly a great variation from the uniform. Indeed, at first instance, the Employment Tribunal held there was insufficient justification for the policy.

Eweida concerns the structurally simple situation of a right and restrictions on that right. Other claims involve the more complex situation of two clashing rights. These are often some of the most difficult and controversial claims to adjudicate. At present, the most frequent clash with the right to manifest a religious belief is the right to non-discrimination, particularly on the grounds of sexual orientation, an issue of contention both within religions and externally. These disputes are not easily resolved. Within our legal system, both rights are important and neither is absolute. Neither right can automatically take preference over the other, partly because there is little societal consensus about the boundary of either right and also because the contexts in which they apply are extremely diverse.

One of the major and continuing areas of this dispute concerns the differences between some religious interpretations of marriage and the opposing demand for marriage or civil partnerships of same-sex couples. This difference can give rise to a number of conflicts. In *Ladele v Islington LBC*,[13] a registrar was dismissed because she refused to perform civil partnerships due to her religious beliefs.

A similar case arose in Saskatchewan in Canada. Following a number of cases at lower levels regarding marriage commissioners[14] who had refused to perform same-sex marriages, a reference was made in the *Marriage Commissioners Case*[15] to the Saskatchewan Court of Appeal (the highest Saskatchewan court). This had a dual purpose: firstly, to consider whether granting an exemption was necessary under the Canadian Charter of Rights and Freedoms and, secondly, to ask whether amending the law to provide a right for marriage commissioners to opt-out of same-sex marriages would be compliant with the Charter. In both *Ladele* and the *Marriage Commissioners Case*, the courts reached the same decision: that there was no right to refuse to perform such ceremonies. What is interesting for current purposes is the use of proportionality in the Canadian case compared to the British example.

Ladele was unsuccessful mainly because the British courts, following the approach taken by the ECtHR, have considered the right to manifest religion within employment to be very limited.[16] Employees are deemed to have accepted all the terms of employment (even though on the facts of this case civil partnerships did not exist when Ladele began working) and as they can resign, so the argument goes, their rights to manifest their religion are maintained. The other reason, given by the Court of Appeal, is that Ladele was under a legal duty not to discriminate. The duty to provide a non-discriminatory service on the grounds of sexual orientation under the Equality Act 2010, applies not only to an organisation as a whole, but also to all individuals working for it.[17] This means that there is no space for a proportionality analysis to take place. No matter how serious the impact of the policy to Ladele or how practically easy it would have been for Islington Council to accommodate her while providing an uninterrupted service to same-sex couples, these concerns could not even be considered. This argument decides that not only was Islington under no obligation to accommodate her but that, once she had been designated a civil partnership registrar, it would have been illegal for them to do so.

By contrast, in the *Marriage Commissioners Case* the Saskatchewan Court considered a number of factors, including: the importance of religious freedom and non-discrimination within the context of the legal system, the particular nature of the job of the marriage commissioner, and the effect a denial of service would have. It was not fatal that the claim was made within employment, although the nature of the employment – that of a public official with direct contact with the public (unlike registrars, marriage commissioners are approached directly by couples to arrange a marriage) – was extremely important. However, this discussion was careful not to morph into a general discussion of the right or wrongness of discriminatory religious beliefs.[18] Instead, both sides' claims, the sincere belief in the sanctity and distinctiveness of opposite-sex marriage and the wish to act in accordance with this *and* the strong interest in being able freely to seek public services without the fear of refusal, were accepted and valued.

In conclusion, the Court held that there was a "less restrictive means" of upholding the right to religious freedom than granting an exemption in the current system. A system could be devised where all couples would apply to a central system and then be assigned a marriage commissioner able and willing to perform the ceremony. Under this system, same-sex couples would not directly face rejection and it would thus be a lesser interference with their rights, but the right to freedom of religion would be upheld. The case, therefore, failed at this point. However, the court went on to consider the next stage of the test even though this was not strictly necessary. It held that when the conflicting interests were balanced, there was not sufficient justification for a religious exemption to be granted in the current system.

A proportionality approach, therefore, does not mean that religion always wins. In fact, in some cases it may lessen religious organisational autonomy since it makes it difficult for religious organisations to create large "islands of exclusivity".[19] This is because there are few absolute answers; each case requires balancing the particular considerations relating to the situation afresh. Blanket policies are, generally, harder to justify than flexible ones. It certainly requires religious practices to be accommodated where this is possible without undermining other goals too greatly. However, it also requires serious consideration of rights claims that may contradict the right to religious autonomy, such as the right to non-discrimination.

Proportionality thus provides a nuanced and theoretically sound method of adjudication. It is not, though, a magic answer to these problems, and can only be one tool among many. Questions as to the appropriate extent of religious exemptions from generally applicable laws or rules, especially where these exemptions affect other rights, are controversial and will remain so for the foreseeable future. There is no way of avoiding difficult decisions. It would, though, be a mistake always to focus on legal solutions. Sometimes even where the issue is at heart a legal one, practical solutions may be available which can adequately protect rights on both sides without requiring legal disputes.[20] If, however, this is not possible or suitable, then a policy of proportionality should be adopted.

references

1   See A. Barak, *Proportionality: Constitutional Rights and their Limitations* (Oxford: Oxford University Press, 2012) chapter 7.

2   See A. Brady, *Proportionality and Deference under the UK Human Rights Act: An Institutionally Sensitive Approach* (Oxford: Oxford University Press, 2012)

3   *Benner v Canada* (Secretary of State) [1997] 1 S.C.R. 358

4   R. Rorty, 'Religion as a Conversation Stopper' in *Philosophy and Social Hope* (London: Penguin, 1999).

5   A. Stone Sweet, and J. Mathews, 'Proportionality, Balancing and Global Constitutionalism', *Columbia Journal of Transnational Law* 47 (2008) p. 73.

6   *Horev v Minister of Transportation*[1997] IsrSC 51(4) 1 English translation available at http://www.ipsofactoj.com/international/2005A/Part03/int2005A%2803%29-009.htm Accessed 10 July 2012

7   D. M. Beatty, *The Ultimate Rule of Law* (Oxford University Press, 2004) pp. 58-60.

8   M. Cohen-Eliya and I. Porat, 'Proportionality and the Culture of Justification' *American Journal of Comparative Law* 59 (2011) pp. 463, 471.

9   Equality Act 2010 s.19.

10 *R (Williamson) v Secretary of State for Education and Employment* [2005] UKHL 15.

11 *Eweida v British Airways Plc* [2010] EWCA Civ 80.

12 At para 22 quoting *Kalaç v Turkey* (1997) 27 EHRR 552.

13 *Ladele v Islington LBC* [2009] EWCA Civ 1357.

14 Marriage commissioners are licenced by the provincial authorities to perform marriages. They are not paid a salary but instead are paid a fixed fee by the couple to perform a marriage. In Saskatchewan, the Marriage Unit maintains a list of marriage commissioners but a couple is responsible for finding a commissioner willing and able to perform their ceremony themselves.

15 *Marriage Commissioners* (2011) SKCA 3.

16 E.g. *Copsey v WBB Devon Clays Ltd* [2005] I.C.R 1789. See T. J. Gunn, 'Adjudicating Rights of Conscience under the European Convention on Human Rights' in J. D. van der Vyver and J. Witte (eds.), *Religious Human Rights in Global Perspective: Legal Perspectives* (The Hague: Martinus Nijhoff, 1996); J. Dingemans, 'The Need for a Principled Approach to Religious Freedoms' 12 (2010) *Ecclesiastical Law Journal* p. 371.

17 Equality Act 2010 s.29.

18 Discriminatory is here used in a neutral sense. No moral judgment should be inferred.

19 A. Esau, 'Islands of Exclusivity': Religious Organizations and Employment Discrimination' *UBC Law Review* 33 (2000) p. 719.

20 See M. Minow 'Should Religious Groups be Exempt from Civil Rights Law?' *Boston College Law Review* 48 (2007) p. 781; J. Gerarda Brown 'Peacemaking in the Culture War Between Gay Rights and Religious Liberty', *Iowa Law Review* 95 (2010) p. 747.

paying for another's belief: the law on indirect religious discrimination

The Equality Act 2010 designates "religion or belief" a "protected characteristic". The Act protects people in respect of all such characteristics from both direct and indirect discrimination. A discriminates against B *directly* if "A treats B less favourably than A treats or would treat others."[1] An employer is, for example, guilty of direct religious discrimination if he refuses to employ or promote a Muslim because he is a Muslim. A discriminates against B *indirectly* if A applies to B "a provision, criterion or practice" (PCP) that disadvantages people who shares B's characteristic, even though the disadvantage may be an incidental and unintended consequence of the PCP. If, for example, an employer has a dress code for his employees and if it is more difficult for Muslims than for others to comply with that dress code, he is guilty, prima facie, of indirect religious discrimination (IRD). He can, however, escape the charge of IRD if he can show that his PCP is "a proportionate means of achieving a legitimate aim."[2]

The claim that direct discrimination, including direct religious discrimination, is unfair is unlikely to be challenged. The claim that indirect discrimination, particularly indirect religious discrimination, is unfair is altogether more controversial. Consider the following case.

Sarah Desrosiers owned and ran a small hairdressing salon in North London, named 'Wedge'. She advertised for an assistant stylist and Bushra Noah applied for the position. Noah was a Muslim who wore a headscarf that covered her hair entirely. That itself was not for Desrosiers an obstacle to her employing Noah. However, during the course of an interview, Desrosiers discovered that Noah would refuse to remove her headscarf while she was working in the salon. That was a problem for Desrosiers, since she required the hair-styles of her hairdressers to be visible to the salon's customers. Her salon offered an "alternative" form of hair dressing, which she described as "ultra-modern" and "urban, edgy and funky". She wanted her hairdressers to use their own hair to model the salon's style (a practice common in hair salons in Britain). Because Noah was unwilling to comply with that practice, Desrosiers did not offer her the position. Noah responded by registering a claim of unlawful discrimination against Desrosiers.

An Employment Tribunal heard the case during Spring 2008. Noah claimed she had been subject to both direct and indirect discrimination. The Tribunal dismissed her claim of direct discrimination, but decided her claim of indirect discrimination was well-founded. Desrosiers' practice of requiring her employees to show their hair placed female Muslims, who, like Noah, wore a headscarf for religious reasons, at a disadvantage compared with those who adhered to other faiths or to none. Moreover, the Tribunal decided that Desrosiers had not shown that her PCP, requiring employees to reveal their hair, was "a proportionate means of achieving a legitimate aim".[3] Noah claimed compensation of £34,000. The Tribunal awarded her £4,000 in respect of "injury to feelings". Of greater moment for Desrosiers was the estimated £40,000 she had to sacrifice in preparing for the trial and the prospect of bankruptcy.[4]

How should we view the outcome of this case? Was it a triumph for fairness, since it upheld Noah's right not to be deprived of an employment opportunity because of her religious faith? Or was it an injustice, since it deprived Desrosiers of the right to run her business according to her own preferred (and not unreasonable) practice, simply because that practice did not suit a religious believer whose beliefs Desrosiers did not share?

The answer to those questions depends in large part on where we should place the responsibility for the situation in which Noah found herself. Was Desrosiers at fault for having a PCP that did not accommodate Noah's religion, or should Noah have borne the 'cost' of complying with her religious belief rather than export that cost to someone else?[5]

choice, responsibility and belief

People's religious beliefs, it is often claimed, differ from their race or gender in being chosen and they warrant different treatment because they are chosen. We are unlikely to find that claim persuasive in relation to direct discrimination; even if people do choose their beliefs, we are unlikely to accept that, as a consequence, they should be open to direct discrimination in employment and in their access to goods and services. But choice may well make a difference to our thinking on IRD. If my chosen beliefs clash with an employer's practice, why should it fall to the employer to bear the costs of my choice? People cannot reasonably expect to choose without bearing the consequences of their choice. If my choice renders me less eligible for employment, I should not be able to offload the cost of that choice onto an employer.

So can people be said to choose their beliefs? The notion that they do runs into two objections. First, people cannot choose what to believe; they can believe only what appears to them to be the case. I cannot choose to believe that Madrid is in France rather than Spain and I cannot choose to believe that the earth is flat rather than spherical. Secondly, the notion that people choose their religious beliefs flies in the face of sociological reality. For most of the world's population, religious belief is a consequence of family or community socialisation. Catholic communities beget Catholics and Muslim societies beget Muslims. Of course, that is not true without exception but, in the context of the world's believing population, converts into and out of faiths constitute a tiny minority.

The first of these objections is less than conclusive. Choices do not have to be arbitrary to be real. I may have reason to pursue a career in law rather than medicine and that reason may outweigh all reasons to the contrary, but my career in law can still be 'chosen'. Moreover, since religious belief is underdetermined by evidence, it is clearly different in character from belief that Madrid is in Spain or that the earth is spherical. There is scope for epistemic discretion in matters of religious belief, even though the language of 'choice' is too gauche to describe that discretion appropriately. If there were no discretion, the idea of 'freedom of belief' would make little sense. (Compare the oddity of 'freedom of race' or 'freedom of gender'.)

The second objection is harder to gainsay. It is just a fact about our world that, for the great majority of religious believers, the social context in which they have developed has been the principal determinant of their religious belief. That is one reason why the phenomena of religion and culture are so closely associated. Should this feature of religious belief preclude our requiring people to take responsibility for what they believe and for the consequences of their belief?

Arguably, it matters less how people have come to hold their beliefs than how they now regard them. There may be a large element of inheritance in their beliefs but, if they now embrace and endorse those beliefs, they cannot present them to others as burdens with which they have been saddled by circumstance and for which they should receive compensation. The reality is, of course, that people do not present their beliefs to others in that way. They hold that others should take their beliefs seriously because they take them seriously; it is because they embrace and endorse their beliefs that others must respect their beliefs. So the claims that the religious make upon others in respect of their beliefs are typically grounded in their strong identification with their beliefs, not in the complaint that their beliefs are burdensome misfortunes with which they have been saddled by the past and for which they should take no responsibility. They are wise to do so, since the 'burdensome misfortune' complaint would invite others not to take seriously the beliefs of the complainers.

The principle of freedom of belief involves the notion that your beliefs are 'none of my business'. It does, of course, leave me free to make my own assessment of your beliefs. But, even if I assess your beliefs as bizarre, implausible, heretical, benighted, or lacking merit in some other way, the principle debars my impeding or interfering with your freedom to hold and pursue whatever beliefs you possess. But if your beliefs become a source of positive rather than merely negative claims against me, so that I have, for example, to give up resources or adjust my behaviour out of deference to your belief, your belief does reasonably become 'my business'. If your belief is going to impose positive obligations on me, it is entirely reasonable that I should judge it and, if I find it wanting, dismiss it as a reason for my having those positive obligations.

We can add the more general point that freedom of belief is supposed to work both ways round: it is freedom to embrace and freedom to reject a belief. If X's embracing p is reason for Y's incurring positive obligations with respect to X, why should that reason not be cancelled by Y's believing in *not-p*? Why should my belief that Christ was the Son of God count for more than your belief that he was not; and why should your belief that Mohammed was God's Prophet count for more than my belief that he was not? After all, we find it no more acceptable that people should be made to comply with religious beliefs they reject than that they should be prevented from complying with religious beliefs they accept.

A final consideration is the way the courts deal with religious belief. Their practice is to refrain from subjecting religious beliefs to any sort of test of plausibility, reasonableness, or orthodoxy. They do subject claims of belief to a sincerity test and they will not protect manifestations of belief that are inconsistent with 'basic standards of human dignity and integrity'.[6] But, within those broad limits, courts do not subject the content of beliefs to any form of quality control. It is entirely appropriate that they should not; courts are not the right bodies to rule on abstruse and contentious points of theology. But if a legal system leaves the religious beliefs that people are free to embrace and pursue so comprehensively free of quality control, if it imposes no check upon their plausibility or reasonableness, it is hard to accept that a believer, merely in virtue of embracing a belief, should be able to impose positive obligations upon others.

beliefs and consequences

The considerations marshalled in the previous section argue strongly for requiring people to take responsibility for their beliefs and for the demands of their beliefs. But they relate to only half the picture. There are consequences of belief that we can regard as uniquely consequences of belief, such as the Christian sabbatarian's having to forgo the recreational activities in which others engage on Sundays or the Muslim's having to devote time to praying five times a day. But the consequences at stake in IRD are not of that kind. They are consequences that arise from the intersection of belief with a social arrangement that is external to the belief. For example, Bushra Noah ran into problems not merely because her religion required her to cover her hair but because that requirement, in combination with Sarah Desrosiers' practice of requiring her hairdressers to show their hair, precluded her gaining employment in Desrosiers' salon. Her failure to gain employment was not uniquely a consequence of her belief; it was the joint consequence of her belief and Desrosiers' practice. We might, therefore, hold Noah and Desrosiers jointly responsible for Noah's predicament or assign primary responsibility to Desrosiers.

If people are to take responsibility for their belief, it follows that a society should provide for the distribution of freedom and resources amongst its citizens without reference to the different beliefs of different believers. So we might imagine a society first establishing a basic structure of freedoms and making provision (through the market or other mechanisms) for the distribution of resources; it will then leave citizens at liberty to use their freedom and resources to pursue their beliefs as they see fit. The demands of people's particular beliefs should not dictate the freedoms or the resources to which they are entitled.

Consider, for example, believers who subscribe to faiths that require them to go on pilgrimages and to construct places of worship such as churches, temples, mosques, and synagogues. The approach I have proposed will require them to fund pilgrimages and places of worship from their own resources, rather than, say, through public taxation that would oblige those who do not share the relevant beliefs to contribute to the costs of those religious endeavours. This may seem nothing like the case of indirect discrimination, but it is to the extent that it is not their beliefs alone that oblige the religious to devote resources to pilgrimages and religious buildings. It is also the fact that those who provide travel services and construct buildings charge for materials and labour at the going rates. Thus, the expense incurred by believers is not uniquely a consequence of their belief; it is a consequence of the intersection of their beliefs with a social arrangement concerning the provision of goods and services. We could, therefore, hold that, since believers' having to pay for pilgrimages and buildings is not a state of affairs produced by the believers alone but is jointly brought about by the believers, on the one hand, and the suppliers of goods and services on the other, the two parties should share joint responsibility for the 'consequence'. The believers should pay half the cost and the suppliers should bear the other half or perhaps receive it in the form of a public subsidy provided by society at large. That proposal is unlikely to find favour with anyone. It is perfectly true that believers are not the only agents responsible for the costs of going on pilgrimages and constructing places of worship; but, provided the believers have been treated in the same way as others in the background system for allocating resources, it will be fair that they should bear those costs and not export them to others.

Where does that leave the case for making legal provision against IRD? There is one feature of existing British law that is congruent with what I have argued above. As previously indicated, a PCP used by an employer or provider of goods and services does not fall foul of discrimination law if it is "a proportionate means of achieving a legitimate aim". The spirit of that provision is that people should not be prevented by the beliefs of others from pursuing the normal aims of normal organisations, or from doing so in ways that are clearly appropriate to those aims. Up to the threshold set by the proportionality criterion, the employer or provider is obliged to accommodate the believer but, once that criterion is met, the wish of the employer or provider prevails. Thus, the proportionality test functions, or should function, as a priority rule in which an organisation's 'normal activity' trumps the competing claims of a believer.

It is well to remember that this priority rule applies not just to business organisations whether they are large corporations or small businesses like Sarah Desrosiers'. It applies to any organisation that is an employer or a provider of goods or services, including government departments, government agencies, local authorities, charities, schools, and universities. Its spirit also applies to religious organisations. The law allows religious organisations to discriminate on grounds of religious belief, within limits, in employment and in the provision of goods and services and it would be absurd if it did not. It also allows organised religions to discriminate on grounds of gender and sexual orientation insofar as compliance with their doctrines and the strongly held convictions of their followers requires that discrimination. I shall not pause to consider the details here.[7] I draw attention only to the fact that the discrimination law governing organised religions and other religious organisations embodies the same principle that an organisation should not be prevented by obligations to accommodate others from pursuing its core aims through proportionate means.

providing against indirect religious discrimination

Is there then a case for combating IRD at all? There are several considerations, other than those that have been my central concern, that bear on the case for IRD legislation. One is the need to provide against covert direct discrimination. Another is the desirability of weeding out practices that disadvantage the religious for no good reason; practices that may have been costless in a largely mono-faith society may not remain so once the religious make-up of the society changes. A third is the social issues that we run into when religious differences track ethnic divisions, as they do in Britain and many other European societies, so that religious disadvantage compounds racial disadvantage.

These considerations argue powerfully for some legal provision against IRD. However, I do not mean to rely on them to the exclusion of the consideration that has been my primary concern: the claims that people have simply as conscientious bearers of religious belief.

Freedom of belief requires that people should not be prevented from living in accordance with their beliefs. If we are committed to that freedom, it is entirely intelligible that we should regret clashes between the demands of a religious belief and a society's public or private arrangements that result in believers being 'burdened' in ways that other people are not. Such burdens may not deprive people of freedom of belief strictly speaking, but they are a form of cost or disadvantage and we may reasonably regret that people's religious beliefs should be a source of social disadvantage for them. A society committed to freedom of belief can therefore reasonably wish to mitigate the burdens that people incur when beliefs clash with its public or private arrangements, insofar as that mitigation is reasonable. But we are then left with the question of what sort or degree of mitigation is 'reasonable'. My answer is: mitigation that does not impose significant costs upon others.[8] That is also the answer implicit in the test that provides a legal defence against claims of IRD: whether the "provision, criterion or practice" at issue is a proportionate means for achieving a legitimate aim. If a PCP fails that test, the implication is that it can be set aside without significant cost to the employer or provider.

It remains important, however, that the proportionality test should be conceived in the right way. The thrust of my argument is that it should be conceived as a priority rule that sets a threshold rather than as a balancing rule that weighs competing interests. The proportionality of the employer's or provider's means (his PCP) should be judged in relation to his aim, provided the aim is 'legitimate'; if the means so judged is proportionate, that should trump the competing claim of the believer. The test should not be one in which the interest of the believer is weighed against that of the employer or provider and the proportionality of the PCP is made to turn on the relative weight of the interests at stake.

Frequently, when courts apply a test of proportionality in other areas of law, they adopt a balancing approach and that approach has sometimes been used by Tribunals dealing with cases of IRD. Indeed, it figured in the Tribunal's assessment in *Noah v. Desrosiers*.[9] What I have argued here challenges the rightness of that approach. Rather, we should begin by assessing the legitimacy of the employer's or provider's aim. If it is legitimate, we should judge the proportionality of the means (the PCP) solely in terms of that aim. If accommodating the wish of the believer is consistent with proportionate means so judged, it should be accommodated; if it is not, it should not be accommodated.

references

1   Equality Act 2010, Pt 2, ch. 2, s.13.

2   Equality Act 2010, Pt 2, ch. 2, s.19.

3   My account of *Noah v. Desrosiers* is based on details given in the (unreported) judgment of the Employment Tribunal, case number 2201867/2007. The case preceded the Equality Act 2010 and was pursued under the Employment Equality (Religion or Belief) Regulations 2003, but, for the most part, the substance of those Regulations remains unchanged in the Equality Act 2010.

4   Report, including an interview with Desrosiers, *Mail Online*, 18 June 2008, http://www.dailymail.co.uk/femail/article-1027300/How-I-nearly-lost-business-refusing-hire-Muslim-hair-stylist-wouldnt-hair.html Accessed 1 August 2012.

5   The issues raised by IRD share something in common with those raised by 'exemptions', such as the well-known exemption enjoyed by turban-wearing Sikhs from the law that requires motorcyclists to wear crash helmets. However, a significant difference is that, in the case of exemptions, it is the state or society at large that does the accommodating whereas, in the case of IRD, the obligation to accommodate falls upon a particular member of civil society.

6   *R (Williamson) v Secretary of State for Education and Employment* [2005] UKHL 15, at para 23.

7   The relevant parts of the Equality Act 2010 are schedule 3 atpara. 29; schedule 9 at paras 2 and 3; schedule 23 at para 2. See also Russell Sandberg, *Law and Religion* (Cambridge: Cambridge University Press, 2011), pp. 117-128.

8   The language of 'costs' applies to many cases of indirect religious discrimination only in a highly figurative sense. For example, in *Ladele v. London Borough of Islington* – a case in which a registrar sought exemption from her employer's requirement to officiate at civil partnership ceremonies, since she believed that actively participating in enabling same sex unions was contrary to her Christian faith – Islington Council conceded that it could fully employ Ladele in other tasks and without anyone having to forego a civil partnership; to that extent, it could accommodate her request entirely without cost. Nevertheless, the Council, the Employment Appeal Tribunal and the Court of Appeal deemed that immaterial; the relevant consideration was that accommodating Ladele's request would be (they held) inconsistent with the Council's 'Dignity for All' policy. *Lillian Ladele v. London Borough of Islington*, [2008] UKEAT/0453/08/RN; [2009] EWCA Civ 1357.

9   *Noah v. Desrosiers* [2008], Employment Tribunal judgment, case number 2201867/2007 at para.160: "the function of the legislation, in its application to indirect discrimination, is to outlaw particular means of pursuing what may be found, in principle, to be entirely legitimate aims, *because of their disproportionately discriminatory impact*" (my emphasis). The Employment Tribunal in *Eweida v. British Airways*, commented, "We do not consider that the blanket ban on everything classified as jewellery struck the correct *balance* between corporate consistency, individual need and accommodation of diversity"; quoted in *Eweida v. British Airways* [2010] Civ 80, para. 32 (my emphasis). In addition, Lucy Vickers has suggested that the number of individuals affected by a requirement might be taken into account in assessing proportionality; 'Religious Discrimination in the Workplace: an Emerging Hierarchy?' *Ecclesiastical Law Journal*, 12 (2010) pp. 280-303, at pp. 289-90.

a question of belief

introduction

One of the most iconic characters in Douglas Adams' *Dirk Gently's Holistic Detective Agency* is the Electric Monk.[1] Describing it as a "labour-saving device" akin to a dishwasher, Adams wrote that the function of Electric Monks was to believe things for people, "saving you what was becoming an increasingly onerous task, that of believing all the things the world expected you to believe."[2] However, the Electric Monk who appears in the novel had developed a fault in that "it had started to believe all kinds of things, more or less at random." Although it thought that its beliefs were unshakeable and would last forever, sometimes new data would lead to new beliefs which overturned previous ones.

The experiences of the character neatly underline the two main problems associated with protecting beliefs: first, the large range of beliefs that might come under such protection; and second, the fact that people may change their beliefs over time in both major and minor ways. These dual problems, of range and change, have come to the fore recently in English discrimination law which now prohibits discrimination on grounds of religion or belief.[3] This essay examines recent employment tribunal cases which have grappled with the definition of belief and suggests a possible way forward.

the changing definition of belief in discrimination law

the original definition: the similar requirement

Although the original EU Framework Directive which forbade discrimination on grounds of religion or belief gave no further definition of the terms 'religion' or 'belief',[4] the definitions of these terms in the domestic legislation giving effect to this Directive originally defined 'religion or belief' as meaning "any religion, religious belief, or similar philosophical belief".[5] The use of the word 'similar' was originally used to exclude certain non-religious beliefs.[6] In *Williams v South Central Limited*[7], an employment tribunal excluded national beliefs, dismissing a claim on the basis that loyalty to a national flag was not included under the Regulations or the dictionary definition of 'belief'.[8] Similarly, in *Baggs v Fudge*[9], a tribunal excluded political beliefs from protection on the basis that they were not similar to religious beliefs. Membership of the British National Party (BNP) did not come under the definition of "similar philosophical belief". 'Religion or belief' meant, in effect, religion or religious-like philosophical belief.

the new definition: removal of the word 'similar' but not the requirement?

Since 2006, the definition of belief has changed.[10] The word 'similar' has been deleted and lack of belief is now expressly included.[11] Belief is now defined as "any religious or philosophical belief".[12] It appears that the reason for the deletion of the word 'similar' was to appease those who professed non-religious beliefs who objected to their beliefs being regarded as being religion-like.

Baroness Scotland, the then Government Minister, claimed that the deletion would make no difference because:

> the term 'philosophical belief' will take its meaning from the context in which it appears; that is, as part of the legislation relating to discrimination on the grounds of religion or belief. Given that context, philosophical beliefs must always be of a similar nature to religious beliefs...it will be for the courts to decide what constitutes a belief...but case law suggests that any philosophical belief must attain a certain level of cogency, seriousness, cohesion and importance, must be worthy of respect in a democratic society and must not be incompatible with human dignity. Therefore an example of a belief that might meet this description is humanism, and examples of something that might not...would be support of a political party or a belief in the supreme nature of the Jedi Knights.[13]

However, a series of employment tribunal decisions have proved the Baroness to be wrong.

the effect of the new definition

The removal of the word 'similar' does appear to have made a difference. And, ironically, the Baroness' explanation of why the law has not changed has itself prompted two changes in approach.

The first relates to her comment that "case law suggests that any philosophical belief must attain a certain level of cogency, seriousness, cohesion and importance, must be worthy of respect in a democratic society and must not be incompatible with human dignity." These words, which originate from Strasbourg jurisprudence, have led employment tribunals to seek inspiration from the case law of the European Convention on Human Rights to develop a definition of belief.

The second change results from the Baroness' example that "support of a political party" was "something that might not" meet the definition. The uncertainty expressed in the word "might" and her explicit reference to "support of a political party", rather than to holding political beliefs per se, have led tribunal chairs to speculate that some political beliefs may now be protected.

In short, the removal of the 'similar' requirement has led to greater attention being afforded to the definition of the word 'belief', and has led to a confused case law. The then government's view that the removal of the word 'similar' would have no effect was naive. It deprived tribunal chairs of the (admittedly crude) methodology that they had developed for determining where the line was to be drawn – namely, by asking whether it was 'similar' to a religious belief or not – without providing any guidance as to what approach was to be taken instead.

The remainder of this essay will look at the confused and inconsistent approach to the definition of belief that has been taken by employment tribunals. However, this requires us to understand what the Strasbourg case law has said about the definition of belief and how that case law has been relied upon by employment tribunal chairs.

the adoption of the Strasbourg jurisprudence

Grainger PLC v Nicholson and the five requirements

The turning point was the decision of the Employment Appeal Tribunal in Grainger PLC v Nicholson,[14] which concluded that an asserted belief in man-made climate change, together with the alleged resulting moral imperatives arising from it, was capable of constituting a 'philosophical belief' because it met the criteria laid out by the European Court of Human Rights' case law on Article 9, which was directly relevant. Mr Justice Burton summarised the Strasbourg definition of 'philosophical belief' as including five requirements:

(1) The belief must be genuinely held.

(2) It must be a belief and not…an opinion or viewpoint based on the present state of information available.

(3) It must be a belief as to a weighty and substantial aspect of human life and behaviour.

(4) It must attain a certain level of cogency, seriousness, cohesion and importance.

(5) It must be worthy of respect in a democratic society, be not incompatible with human dignity and not conflict with the fundamental rights of others.[15]

Although these five requirements can be found in the case law of the Strasbourg court, it would be incorrect to assume that this represents a watertight definition of belief on the part of the European Court of Human Rights. This can be shown by looking briefly at the Strasbourg case law and domestic decisions concerning the definition of belief under human rights law.

the Strasbourg approach

As with other international human rights treaties which seek to protect "religion or belief",[16] a largely pragmatic approach has been taken to the interpretation of Article 9 of the European Convention on Human Rights. Although it is agreed that the ambit extends beyond religion, it remains unclear how far protection has been extended.[17] Generally, the terms have been 'broadly construed' and have been understood as covering "theistic, non-theistic and atheistic beliefs, as well as the right not to profess any religion or belief."[18] The Strasbourg institutions have considered claims concerning scientology,[19] Nazism,[20] druidism,[21] pacifism,[22] communism,[23] atheism,[24] pro-life,[25] Divine Light Zentrum,[26] the Moon Sect,[27] as well as 'splinter' groups within larger traditions,[28] without questioning whether such claims fit the definition of religion or belief.[29] The approach, in short, has been to consider all claims, determining their success on their merits.

A line has been drawn, however, to exclude beliefs that are mere opinions rather than a worldview. As the Office for Democratic Institutions and Human Rights has noted, the term belief "typically pertains to deeply held conscientious beliefs that are fundamental about the human condition and the world."[30] However, Strasbourg has been more than a little vague about what this actually means.

In *Campbell and Cosans v United Kingdom*,[31] it was noted that the term 'convictions' used in Article 2 of the first protocol to the ECHR[32] was "akin" to the term 'beliefs' as used in Article 9, and "denotes views that attain a certain level of cogency, seriousness, cohesion and importance", and could be contrasted with "the words 'opinions' and 'ideas'" found in Article 10.[33] These comments, together with assertions that the term 'convictions' denotes "such convictions as are worthy of respect in a 'democratic society' and are not incompatible with human dignity",[34] are as far as Strasbourg institutions have gone in providing an elucidation of what is meant by the requirement that a belief must be a worldview.

the approach of the domestic human rights case law

These statements have been developed in the domestic human rights case law but even there a cautious approach has been taken. As Lord Nicholls noted in *Williamson*,[35] "a belief must satisfy some modest, objective minimum requirements," namely:

> The belief must be consistent with basic standards of human dignity or integrity. The belief must relate to matters more than merely trivial. It must possess an adequate degree of seriousness and importance. As has been said, it must be a belief on a fundamental problem.[36]

Moreover, for Lord Nicholls, the "belief must also be coherent in the sense of being intelligible and capable of being understood."[37] A non-religious belief "must relate to an aspect of human life or behaviour of comparable importance to that normally found with religious beliefs."[38] However, his Lordship stressed that these "threshold requirements should not be set at a level which would deprive minority beliefs of the protection they are intended to have under the Convention." He noted that "too much should not be demanded in this regard":

> Depending on the subject matter, individuals cannot always be expected to express themselves with cogency or precision. Nor are an individual's beliefs fixed and static. The beliefs of every individual are prone to change over his lifetime.[39]

Lord Walker also doubted whether it was right for courts, except in extreme cases, "to impose an evaluative filter" at the stage of identifying whether there was a belief.[40] As Lord Walker noted, for "the Court to adjudicate on the seriousness, cogency and coherence of theological beliefs is…to take the Court beyond its legitimate role."[41] The definition of belief was not used to determine the case.

However, although Lord Nicholls in *Williamson* stressed that "freedom of religion protects the subjective belief of an individual",[42] a later decision of the House of Lords seemed to adopt a more objective test in relation to defining belief. In *Whaley v Lord Advocate*,[43] concerning the hunting ban, Lord Hope of Craighead rejected the appellant's contention that hunting with hounds constituted a non-religious belief as being beneath the *Williamson* threshold, since looking at it "objectively, hunting with hounds is carried on mainly for pleasure and relaxation for those who take part in it." He added:

> The current jurisprudence does not support the proposition that a person's belief in his right to engage in an activity which he carries on for pleasure or recreation, however fervent or passionate, can be equated with beliefs of the kind that are protected by article 9.[44]

However, Lord Hope did not specify what defined "the kind" of beliefs that Article 9 protects. Indeed, generally, the courts have not relied upon the definition of belief to exclude Article 9 claims.

In contrast, however, employment tribunal chairs interpreting new laws prohibiting discrimination on grounds of religion or belief have done exactly that. Since *Grainger PLC v Nicholson*, Burton's five requirements have taken on an elevated importance. Employment tribunal chairs are now applying these requirements as if they were a statutory test, especially in cases concerning political beliefs. This is contrary to the way in which these principles have developed at Strasbourg and how they were understood by the House of Lords in *Williamson*. This has led to a bewildering and unpredictable case law.

a discriminating case law

Greater Manchester Police Authority v Power: the importance of Grainger

A series of employment tribunal decisions have utilised the five requirements laid out in *Grainger PLC v Nicholson*. This is shown most clearly in *Greater Manchester Police Authority v Power*[45] in which the five requirements were used to hold that a belief in spiritualism and life after death and psychic powers was capable of being a 'belief'. Such a belief met the test adopted in *Grainger PLC v Nicholson*: it was worthy of respect in a democratic society and had the necessary cogency, seriousness, cohesion and importance.[46] Moreover, Burton's decision in *Grainger PLC v Nicholson* questioned whether certain political beliefs were now protected. Although Burton suggested that, despite the removal of the word 'similar', it remained necessary for the belief "to have a similar status or cogency to a religious belief",[47] he also suggested that this did not mean that beliefs in political philosophies were automatically excluded:

> As appears from the passage in Hansard, the Attorney General suggested that "support of a political party" might not meet the description of a philosophical belief. That must surely be so, but that does not mean that a belief in a political philosophy or doctrine would not qualify. [A] belief in the political philosophies of Socialism, Marxism, Communism or free-market Capitalism might qualify.[48]

Kelly v Unison: a new rationale for excluding political beliefs

This suggestion that beliefs in a political philosophy or doctrine may constitute a philosophical belief has caused considerable confusion. This was compounded by the decision in *Kelly v Unison*[49] in which it was held that Marxist/ Trotskyite beliefs held by trade union members of the Socialist Party did not constitute a 'philosophical belief'. However, in reaching this decision, Employment Judge Weiniger was reluctant to adopt the distinction made in *Grainger PLC v Nicholson* between "membership of a party on the one hand and political opinions of an individual member on the other",[50] on the basis that a political party is "no more nor less than a group of like minded individuals with a particular political stance."[51]

Weiniger instead proposed that a distinction could be drawn between "political beliefs which involve the objective of the creation of a legally binding structure by power or government regulating others", which are not protected, and the beliefs protected in *Grainger PLC v Nicholson* which "are expressed by his own practice but where he has no ambition to impose his scheme on others."[52] Weiniger found that there was a principled reason based upon freedom of speech to protect the right of individuals to challenge political aims through criticism, scrutiny, censure and satire.[53]

The tribunal further found that if it had been wrong in its construction of the expression 'philosophical belief' as excluding political beliefs, then nevertheless the beliefs did not meet the *Grainger PLC v Nicholson* tests.[54] In particular, the tribunal thought that it would be difficult to characterise the claimants' views as being a worldview rather than an opinion or viewpoint based on the present state of information available.[55] Although the result in *Kelly v Unison* was ultimately the same as in *Baggs v Fudge* in that the particular political beliefs were held not to be protected, the line drawn in *Kelly v Unison* is much more ambiguous. The case law now suggests that some political beliefs may be protected.

Hashman and Maistry: an increasingly generous approach

A number of more recent employment tribunal decisions concerning non-political beliefs have suggested that an increasingly wide definition is being taken. In *Hashman v Milton Park (Dorset) Ltd*[56] it was found that a belief in the sanctity of life, comprising in particular of anti-foxhunting beliefs, constituted a philosophical belief for the purpose of religious discrimination laws. Although the claimant wore clothes containing animal dye and had continued working for the organisation run by supporters for hunting which profited from the proceeds of killing animals for food, Employment Judge Guyner found that this did not mean that the claimant's beliefs lacked coherence. He accepted the claimant's view that he "had to live in the real world" and needed to earn a living, and that the work he was doing was in conformity with his beliefs.[57] Great weight was attached to the fact that the claimant had a general belief in the sanctity of life, and to the strength of his belief. This suggests that determining whether something is a philosophical belief requires a determination of the significance of the belief to the individual claimant rather than a general assessment of where the line is to be drawn. Such an approach would lead to an unpredictable case law and is difficult to square with the decision in *Kelly v Unison*.

The success of the claim in *Hashman* can also be contrasted with the dismissal of the claim in *Whaley v Lord Advocate*.[58] *Hashman* underlines the general trend that the removal of the word 'similar' has led to a broad approach being taken to the definition of belief, apart from in the case of political beliefs. This is further underscored by the employment tribunal decision in *Maistry v The BBC*[59] in which Employment Judge Hughes held that a belief "that public service broadcasting has the higher purpose of promoting cultural interchange and social cohesion" constituted a 'philosophical belief' because it met the *Grainger PLC v Nicholson* tests.[60]

Tellingly, in reaching his conclusion that the asserted belief was cogent, serious, coherent and important, Employment Judge Hughes stated that he did not accept that the belief was a political opinion or based on a political philosophy but commented that "even if it had been, the appellate courts have not yet definitely determined that question."[61] This suggests that the distinctions drawn in *Grainger PLC v Nicholson* and *Kelly v Unison* may not stand. This is hardly surprising.

Paradoxically, although the tribunal decisions seem to have adopted a wide understanding of belief derived from the Strasbourg jurisprudence, they have also constructed a distinction between different forms of political beliefs which is not reflected in the Article 9 case law, which simply recognises that all political beliefs may be protected (although technically one may dispute whether they are protected under Article 9, 10 or 11). Despite the number of tribunal cases concerned with the definition of belief, the law remains confused and inconsistent.

conclusions

The existence and substance of the case law demonstrates the problems associated with protecting beliefs: chiefly, the dual problems of range and change. This was appreciated by the House of Lords in *Williamson*. Their Lordships' speeches provide many pointers that may guide the way ahead. Their reluctance to use the definition of religion or belief to filter out claims under the Human Rights Act 1998 is sound. And the same approach should be used in discrimination law. The removal of the word 'similar' is, therefore, welcome.

However, the way in which Burton's five requirements are increasingly being treated as if they constituted a statutory definition of belief is unfortunate. Employment tribunals are applying principles derived from Strasbourg jurisprudence in a manner that fails to take heed of Lord Nicholls' concern in *Williamson* that "too much should not be demanded in this regard".[62] This is regrettable. The definition of belief is a blunt instrument. By dismissing claims at the outset, courts are likely to aggrieve claimants and perpetuate fears expressed by Baroness Warsi, among others,[63] that a rising tide of 'militant secularisation' is resulting in religion being "sidelined, marginalised and downgraded in the public sphere".[64]

Taking religious rights claims seriously does not mean that all such claims should be successful. However, it does mean that the courts should refrain from placing significant obstacles in the way of such claims which mean that the claim is not examined in its entirety. In short, a *holistic* approach is required. This would require courts to examine the merits and context of cases in their entirety rather than focussing upon semantic questions concerning the scope of religious rights.[65] As Judge Hughes noted in *Maistry v The BBC*, merely recognising that something may be a philosophical belief does not mean that claims will be successful; it simply means that the claim does not fail at the first hurdle. All other aspects of the claim still need to be proved.

> It may well be that the scope of 'philosophical belief' is wide, but it is worth noting that meeting the *Nicholson* test merely establishes that there is a protected characteristic, such that a discrimination complaint may be brought – the real battleground is whether there has been less favourable treatment and, if so, whether it was on grounds of the belief relied on.[66]

This is not to say that the general principles laid out in *Grainger PLC v Nicholson* cannot be helpful. However, in applying those principles care needs to be taken as to what is being measured. At the time in which the original regulations were being formulated, Lord Brennan pointed out that the word 'similar' related "to the quality of the belief, not its nature."[67] This is surely right. It is not the role of the court in religious rights cases to examine questions of theology and doctrine to determine whether they meet expectations regarding the "level of cogency, seriousness, cohesion and importance".

However, determining the quality of a belief is also problematic. It should not simply be a case of measuring the strength of the claimant's conviction. As *Williamson* and *Hashman* underline, beliefs may change over time and their exercise is shaped by the social environment. Recent scholarship in political and social theory has underscored how identity is "negotiated through dialogue, partly overt, partly internal, with others."[68] In determining religious rights claims, there is a need to place emphasis upon *agency*. This requires appreciation of the way in which identities (and therefore beliefs) are constantly being negotiated and re-negotiated in response to internal and external stimuli. In the words of Phillips, it requires an understanding that people are "cultural beings" rather than being "of a culture".[69] As Lord Nicholls noted in *Williamson*, this requires the recognition that "freedom of religion protects the subjective belief of an individual".[70]

This realisation brings us full circle. Although the Electric Monks illustrate the main problems with defining belief, the title of Adams' novel (and the eponymous character's detection method)[71] may provide us with the way forward: a *holistic* approach based on *agency*.

references

1   Douglas Adams, *Dirk Gently's Holistic Detective Agency* (London: Pan Books, 1987).

2   Ibid. p. 3.

3   Equality Act 2010. For a fuller account of religious discrimination law see R. Sandberg, *Law and Religion* (Cambridge: Cambridge University Press, 2011) chapter 6.

4   Council Directive 2000/78/EC

5   Employment Equality (Religion or Belief) Regulations 2003, Reg 2(1).

6   For a fuller account of legal definitions of religion or belief see Sandberg, *Law and Religion*, op. cit., chapter 3.

7   ET, Case Number: 2306989/2003 (16 June 2004).

8   The dictionary definition used was that: "belief is persuasion of the truth of anything or opinion or doctrine or recognition of an awakened sense of a higher being, controlling power or powers and the morality connected therewith, rights of worship or any system of such belief and worship".

9   *Baggs v Fudge* ET, Case Number: 1400114/2005 (23 March 2005).

10   Section 77 of the Equality Act 2006 substituted the new definition of "religion or belief" into the Regulations. See P. Griffith, 'Protecting the Absence of Religious Belief? The New Definition of Religion or Belief in Equality Legislation' *Religion & Human Rights*, 2/3 (2007) p. 149.

11   The express reference to lack of religion and belief has been seen as simply clarifying what was hitherto presumed in the Parliamentary debate: N. de Marco, *Blackstone's Guide to The Employment Equality Regulations 2003* (Oxford: Oxford University Press, 2004) pp. 12-13.

12   This definition is now to be found in the Equality Act 2010, s10.

13   Hansard, HL vol. 673, cols 1109-1110 (13 Jul. 2005).

14   *Grainger PLC v Nicholson* [2009] UKEAT 0219/09/ZT (3 November 2009).

15   Ibid., at para 24.

16   Article 18 of the Universal Declaration on Human Rights 1948 (UDHR), Article 18 of the International Covenant on Civil and Political Rights 1966 (ICCPR) and 1981 Declaration on the Elimination of All Forms of Intolerance and of Discrimination Based on Religion or Belief.

17   See Sandberg, *Law and Religion* op. cit., pp. 49-50.

18   Human Rights Committee, General Comment 22, para 2; *Kokkinakis v Greece* (1994).

19   *X and Church of Scientology v Sweden* (1978).

20   *X v Austria* (1963).

21   *Chappell v United Kingdom* (1987) 53 DR 241.

22   *Arrowsmtih v United Kingdom* (1978).

23   *Hazar, Hazar and Acik v Turkey* (1991).

24   *Angeleni v Sweden* (1986).

25   *Plattform "Ärtzefür das Leben" v Austria* (1985).

26   *Omkarananda and the Divine Light Zentrum v Switzerland* (1981).

27   *X v Austria* (1981).

28   E.g. *Serif v Greece* (1999) (Mufti elected by Mosque congregations in opposition to the Mufti appointed by the Government).

29   However, on occasions Strasbourg will require claimants to prove the *existence* of the religion in question: in *X v UK* (1977), for example, an application from a prisoner who sought to be registered as a follower of Wicca failed on the grounds that the applicant had "not mentioned any facts making it possible to establish the existence of the Wicca religion, what Wicca was and why there was a breach".

30   Guidelines for Review to Legislation Pertaining to Religion or Belief (2004) Section A, Para 3.

31   *Campbell and Cosans v United Kingdom*, (1982).

32   This provides, *inter alia*, that "the State shall respect the right of parents to ensure such education and teaching in conformity with their own religious and philosophical convictions".

33   *Campbell and Cosans* at para 36.

34   Ibid.

35   *R v Secretary of State for Education and Employment and others ex parte Williamson* [2005] UKHL 15.

36   Ibid., at para 23.

37   Ibid., at para 23.

38   Ibid., at para 24.

39   Ibid., at para 23.

40   Ibid., at para 57.

41   Ibid., at para 60. See also Lord Nicholls at para 22.

42   Ibid., at para 22.

43   *Whaley v Lord Advocate* [2007].

44   Ibid., at para 18.

45   *Greater Manchester Police Authority v Power* [2009] EAT 0434/09/DA (12November 2009).

46   At the full employment tribunal hearing Power lost on the merits of the case: ET 2404433/09 (23-24 November 2009).

47   Ibid., at para 26.

48   Ibid., at para 28.

49   *Kelly v Unison* ET 2203854/08 (22 December 2009).

50   Ibid., at para 108.

51   Ibid., at para 109.

52   Ibid., at para 114.

53   Ibid., at para 123.

54   The tribunal noted that there had been "criticism from commentators about the reliance in *Nicholson* on the jurisprudence derived from principles and case law under Article 9" but held that the "adoption of such resources is a matter of convenient re-statement, following principles, reasoned considerations and conclusions…which find merit and resonate in the way in which domestic legislation is to be construed." At para 132.

55   Ibid., at para 129.

56   *Hashman v Milton Park (Dorset) Ltd* ET 3105555/2009 (31 January 2011).

57   Ibid., at para 35. He observed that "Sometimes one's moral decisions cannot be based on a simple set of black and white principles" at para 58.

58   *Whaley v Lord Advocate* [2007]

59   *Maistry v The BBC* ET Pre-Hearing Review Case Number: 1213142/2010 (14 February 2011).

60   Ibid., at para 17-18.

61   Ibid., at para 19.

62   *Williamson* [2005] UKHL 15 at para 23.

63   A recent inquiry by Christians in Parliament (an All-Party Parliamentary Group) concluded that: "Christians in the UK face problems in living out their faith and these problems have been mostly caused and exacerbated by social, cultural and legal changes over the past decade." See the 'Clearing the Ground Inquiry', http://www.eauk.org/clearingtheground.

64   See http://www.bbc.co.uk/news/uk-17021831 and http://www.telegraph.co.uk/news/religion/9080441/We-stand-side-by-side-with-the-Pope-in-fighting-for-faith.html

65   See, further, Sandberg, *Law and Religion* op. cit., chapter 10 and R. Sandberg, 'The Adventures of Religious Freedom' Centre for Law and Religion, Cardiff University, Working Paper series http://www.law.cf.ac.uk/clr/research/WorkingPapers.html

66   *Maistry v The BBC*, at para 20.

67   Hansard, HL vol. 649, col 788 (17 June 2003).

68   C. Taylor, "The Politics of Recognition" in A. Guttmann (ed.), *Multiculturalism: Examining the Politics of Recognition* (Princeton University Press, 1994) p. 25; see also e.g., Z. Bauman, *Liquid Modernity* (Cambridge: Polity Press, 2000).

69   A. Phillips, *Multiculturalism without Culture* (Princeton University Press, 2007) p. 52.

70   *Williamson*, at para 22.

71   D. Adams, *Dirk Gently* op. cit.

is religious freedom special?

American and European views

What, if anything, is special about religious freedom?[1] The question could be understood as asking what is special about religion. In a secular society, intent on treating religion as an essentially private pursuit which may have to be severely constrained, claims to freedom of religion can appear to be mere special pleading by particular interests. Why should a religious conscience be rated as more important than a non-religious one? The European Convention of Human Rights in its Article 9, dealing with 'freedom of thought, conscience and religion' very obviously talks of "religion or belief", widening the area of its protection in a vague manner. The rejection of religion should clearly be included in any understanding of freedom of religion, but adding 'belief' could include vegetarianism, pacifism, environmentalism, or anything a subject takes seriously. The wider the scope, the more manifestations of beliefs may have to be curbed. A narrow definition of religion might on the other hand guarantee some greater protection.

In this, there is a difference between Europe and the United States. The First Amendment to the United States Constitution famously sates that "Congress shall make no law respecting an establishment of religion, or prohibiting the free exercise thereof." In other words, 'religion' is specifically marked out for protection. It is mentioned first in the Bill of Rights, and is often called the 'first freedom', with the added implication that it is of particular importance. Many of the most influential Founders came from Virginia, such as Thomas Jefferson, James Madison, and George Washington himself. They had lived under an Establishment of the Church of England that had paid scant regard to the 1689 Act of Toleration passed by Westminster. Members of other denominations that were growing at the time in the colony, such as Baptists and Presbyterians, felt their freedom to worship was being constricted. Indeed, because the Church of England in Virginia was locally under the control of 'vestries' made up of powerful gentry such as George Washington himself, without a resident Bishop, this was part of a perceived lack of democratic freedom. It was not surprising that religious freedom and wider democratic freedoms were regarded as indissolubly linked in the fledgling United States.

Religion, almost by definition, concerns what is most important in an individual's life. If someone cannot live by those most basic beliefs, and manifest them, they are not truly free. Freedom of worship is itself important, but genuine freedom of religion has to cover more than that, and can influence all of my actions. A restriction on such freedom, and indeed any attempt to force religion into the private life of citizens, totally segregated from their life in the public sphere, is not just an attack on an important element of human life. It is indeed an attack on the very possibility of all democratic freedom.

The split between American and European views about the need to give religion special protection no doubt owes its origin to the differing views of the early and later Enlightenment. John Locke's views of toleration influenced Jefferson, and Locke rooted his views in a theistic view of the world. Human reason for him stemmed from that of God. It was the "candle of the Lord".[2] For the French Enlightenment, however, reason was a liberating force against traditional sources of authority and 'superstition', such as the Roman Catholic Church. Freedom meant freedom *from* religion, not, as was the case in the United States, freedom *for* religion.

an example: the 'ministerial exception'

The more secularist attitude of a country like France influences wider views in Europe of today. Two recent court cases, one in England and the other in the United States illustrate the point. In January 2012, the United States Supreme Court unanimously made what was considered by some to be a landmark judgment in the area of religious freedom. It concerned what is called in the United States the 'ministerial exception', the principle that ministers of religion should be treated differently from other employees. The Court agreed that it is "impermissible for the government to contradict a church's determination of who can act as its ministers".[3] The government, it held, should not interfere with matters that affected the mission of the church. Only the church could decide who should 'personify' its faith. It accepted that society had an interest in eradicating wrongful employment discrimination, but that could not override a church's freedom "to choose who will guide it on its way."

As Justice Alito commented in a supporting opinion, "the autonomy of religious groups, both here in the United States and abroad, has often served as a shield against oppressive civil laws."[4] Churches and other religious institutions act as buffers in civil society between the individual and the state. Indeed, we might add that if the influence of those buffers is removed, it will be inevitable that, without any other restraints on individual behaviour, the state will have to step in and arrogate ever more power to itself.

Yet all this is contrasted with the willingness, in the previous month, of the Court of Appeal in London to overturn a long-standing understanding in Britain that a minister of religion is not an ordinary employee but an 'office-holder', not subject to normal employment law. Instead, it concluded that such ministers were in a contractual arrangement with a church and, as such, subject to normal employment law. The Court cheerfully admitted that it was "fulfilling the time-honoured role of updating the common law and making it more suitable for modern circumstances."[5] More ominously, it referred to Article 9 of the European Convention on Human Rights, concerning religious freedom, and asked rhetorically (and perhaps even contemptuously): "What, it may be asked..., has this to do with the domestic law of unfair dismissal?"[6] In other words, unfair dismissal must be irrelevant to any consideration of religious freedom. Yet that which in secular eyes might be an outrageous example of unfair dismissal, could be regarded as a necessary action according to the spiritual discipline of a church. The issue is whether the state can dictate to churches and other religious organisations how to discipline their own clergy. Churches can then become unable to enforce the standards required by their faith, even though individual ministers might gain a measure of job security. Unlike in the United States, it is apparent that secular standards have been allowed to sweep away any respect for the individual needs of churches as institutions. The state's protection of individual rights does not allow, it seems, any buffer between individual and government.

the narrowing of religious freedom

Freedom of contract in Europe outweighs mere considerations of religious freedom. This is shown at its starkest when people want exemptions for religious reasons from certain duties. To take one example, should someone be free to wear a cross for religious reasons, even if their employer forbids it? Another example concerns whether, say, a civil registrar should be able to opt out of conducting civil partnership ceremonies for religious reasons. In such cases, the British Government's understanding, as given in the 'Respondent's Observations' to the European Court of Human Rights was that "where the individual in question is free to resign and seek employment elsewhere or practise their religion unfettered outside their employment", that is sufficient to guarantee their Article 9 rights in domestic law."[7] That observation follows previous jurisprudence from the European Court that suggests that freedom of contract is enough to guarantee freedom of religion. If you do not like what your job entails, you can give it up. Yet the freedom to be unemployed is not much of a freedom, and the attitude certainly places little special value on religious freedom.

The case of the civil registrar, Lillian Ladele, dismissed from Islington Borough Council for refusing to conduct civil partnerships, illustrates other ways in which religious freedom can be downgraded in the face of different priorities. The Court of Appeal in London supported the "overarching" policy of the London Borough of Islington to outlaw all discrimination on grounds of sexual orientation. The clash is well summed up in one passage of the judgment, where it is said that this policy "had fundamental human rights, equality and diversity implications, whereas the effect on Ms Ladele of implementing the policy did not impinge on her religious beliefs: she remains free to hold those beliefs, and free to worship as she wishes."[8] Thus discrimination on grounds of sexual orientation is made to trump that of discrimination because of religion.

The Court does not see it in that way because it is carefully defining freedom of religion in the narrowest way possible. We are, it seems, absolutely free to hold whatever beliefs we wish as long as we do not manifest them. At least, the idea of manifestation is carefully restricted to the most narrow understanding of religion possible, that of the mere participation in public rituals. Freedom of religion is tacitly redefined as freedom of worship. Even so, however, European jurisprudence does not even uphold that. Since freedom of contract guarantees freedom of religion, no-one can expect consideration from employers to allow attendance at public worship on a Sunday (or Saturday or Friday). They are still free to worship because they do not have to take, or stay in, a job that demands working instead of worshipping.[9] The idea of freedom of religion has been so attenuated that even a totalitarian ruler might be happy with it, as religion is, it seems, not understood as influencing lives.

Religion is being evicted from the public sphere as an influence on public life and is tolerated as a private pursuit of individuals. Some people choose to attend a place of worship on a Sunday morning instead, say, of playing golf. That is as far as it goes. Religion, as such, has no general relevance on the public stage.[10] The importance of 'diversity' is often invoked, but a crucial ingredient of democracy is diversity of opinion. In fact, all ought to be able to bring into public discussion their vision of the common good. Religious views may well be crucial, as they certainly have been in contributing to the formation of policy in the past throughout the Western democracies. They certainly pick out what individuals think is of fundamental importance in human life. Indeed it should be the mark of a functioning democracy that it respects differing views, and upholds the consciences of those holding them. The imposition of any orthodoxy, whether religious or secular, by law and the state strikes at the root of this vision.

religion as 'irrational'?

What lies at the root of this apparent dismissal of religion and its influence? We have already remarked on the anti-religious influence of the later Enlightenment, but the early English Enlightenment, in places such as Cambridge, was theologically based. The Royal Society was founded at the birth of modern science, by men (and they were only men) who, for the most part, had a theological basis for wanting to find out more of the glories of 'Creation'. Other philosophical influences are more recent.

In controversial remarks in a case in the Court of Appeal for England and Wales in 2010, Lord Justice Laws made sweeping observations on the nature of religion as such. They belonged more in a seminar on the philosophy of religion than in a law court, but consisted of a few assertions that were based on no argument.[11] He claimed that "in the eye of everyone save the religious believer religious faith is necessarily subjective, being incommunicable by any kind of proof or evidence." He further said that to use law to protect a position held purely on religious grounds is "irrational, as preferring the subjective over the objective." Thus he swept aside centuries of discussion about the respective roles of faith and reason. As 'subjective' faith is always directed at something which has to be specified, reason must immediately be brought into play. Many books have been written on the rationality of religious belief.[12] The insistence of Lord Justice Laws on 'proof' and 'evidence' might suggest that he is still in thrall to an outmoded logical positivism that linked truth intimately with the possibility of scientific evidence. That does not even stand up to examination in contemporary physics, which revels in the putative existence of purely theoretical entities.[13] The view has, as a consequence, long been discarded in the philosophy of science.

The views of one judge might be discarded as an aberration, but the dicta of Lord Justice Laws are being quoted by other judges with approval in other important cases. They thus risk setting the acknowledged standard for how religion is to be viewed by English law. One such case concerned the wish of Bideford Town Council to continue having prayers at the start of its meetings. It is a historic town and had done so since at least the reign of Elizabeth I. A majority of councillors had on more than one occasion voted to continue the practice. The Judge, however, judged the case on the narrow point of the Council's powers under the Local Government Act of 1972, which empowered a Council to do anything "which is calculated to facilitate, or is conducive or incidental to, the discharge of any of their functions."

Quite properly the Judge commented that "it is not for a Court to rule upon the likelihood of divine, and presumptively beneficial, guidance being available or the effectiveness of Christian public prayer in obtaining it."[14] Yet he was concerned with the notion of equality and the need for "all councillors to participate equally on all matters." Equality for him trumped religious freedom.[15] This might explain why the conclusion he drew from the need to make theological judgments is that the Council did not have the power to hold prayers. Yet historical judgment and the democratic wishes of elected councillors pointed strongly in the opposite direction. If a Court cannot decide whether prayer helps a Council in its business, why should it stop the praying? One reason is clearly the assumption, articulated by Lord Justice Laws, that religion cannot take a full part in democratic, rational discussion. It is basically irrational (and hence even possibly dangerous to the cohesion of society).

If religion is not be allowed a voice in public debates, but is regarded as of only subjective validity, that may go a long way to explaining why freedom of religion is being so circumscribed by the law. Religious freedom is in the wrong sense regarded as special, in that it appears to concern the private tastes of individuals, which can be unpredictable and dangerous. It is not, it seems, something to be cherished for its own sake as an indispensable element in democracy, or something that can be rationally challenged. The law cannot take rational account of it, let alone look to it for any justification of its own practices. Yet this turns the English common law on its head. It becomes subject to the whims of the moment. It is significant that in the case concerning the employment status of a Methodist minister (already referred to), the judges regarded it a virtue that they were "updating" the common law and making it more suitable to modern circumstances.

The common law of England is as steeped in Christian principles as is the history of England entwined with Christianity. In spring 2012, a find was announced near Cambridge of the burial place of a high-ranking Anglo-Saxon teenage girl, dating from about 680 A.D. The significance of the find was that she was wearing a cross. It seemed to be part of her habitual wear, and that, it was said, showed that she was an early Anglo-Saxon Christian. Not only does this say something of the history of Christianity in early England, but it is ironic that it was wearing the cross that clearly marked her as a Christian. In present-day English courts wearing a cross is classed with having a dispensable piece of jewellery. In a case that went on to the European Court of Human Rights an employee of British Airways was told by the Court of Appeal that the visible wearing of a cross was a personal preference. "There was no suggestion," the Court held, "that her religious belief, however profound, called for it."[16] It was not a core belief, as determined by the Court. Yet it is one thing to choose whether or not wear a cross. It is another to be forbidden from doing so.

Arguments over symbols often cloak deeper disputes. Religion in general, and Christianity in particular, is, it seems, not to be brought into public places either symbolically or as part of the democratic debate. Religion has always been vulnerable because it poses an authority different from, and sometimes at odds with, secular authority. Even if that authority is democratic, the 'will of the people', it dislikes being judged by other standards. The vulnerability of religion, both on an institutional and individual basis, is a good reason for giving a special emphasis to freedom of religion. Yet it is also clear that once freedom of contract, freedom of conscience or other freedoms are thought sufficient, religion itself becomes marginalised. The problem is that English law has rested on assumptions about freedom, equality and human dignity that are derived from Christianity. Even if there may be other foundations, it is undeniable that Christianity has helped to nourish these principles. If it is removed from the scene, the question has to be whether everything can long remain the same.

references

1 See also Roger Trigg, *Equality, Freedom and Religion* (Oxford: Oxford University Press, 2012).

2 See John Locke, *An Essay Concerning Human Understanding* Book IV, ch. 3 A. S. Pringle-Pattison (ed.), (Oxford: Oxford University Press, 1924) p. 280. (The 'candle of the Lord' was a phrase much used by the Cambridge Platonists, particularly Benjamin Whichcote, Locke's favourite preacher.)

3 *Hosanna-Tarbor Evangelical Church and School v. Equal Opportunity Commission*, 565 US_ 2012 Slip Opinion, p. 10.

4 Alito J. *Hosanna-Tarbor*, Concurring Opinion, 565 US _ 2012, Slip Op. p. 3.

5 *President of the Methodist Conference v Preston*, (2011) EWCA Civ 1581 para 25.

6 Ibid., para 29.

7 Observations of the Government of the United Kingdom (1) *Nadia Eweida* and (2) *Shirley Chaplin v. United Kingdom*, European Court of Human Rights, App. Nos 48420/10 and 59842/10.

8 *Ladele v. London Borough of Islington* (2009) EWCA Civ 1357 para 51.

9 See my *Religion in Public Life*, (Oxford: Oxford University Press, 2007) pp. 153-60.

10 Ibid.

11 See *McFarlane v Relate Avon Ltd* (2010) EWCA Civ 880, para, 23. Also see my *Equality, Freedom and Religion* pp. 142ff.

12 See, for example, my *Reason and Commitment* (Cambridge: Cambridge University Press, 1973), and *Rationality and Religion: Does Faith Need Reason?* (Oxford: Blackwell Books, 1982).

13 See my *Rationality and Science: Can Science Explain Everything?* (Oxford: Blackwell Books, 1993).

14 *National Secular Society v. Bideford Town Council* (2012) EWHC 175 (Admin) para 29.

15 See my *Equality, Freedom and Religion* to see that this is a recurring theme in contemporary law.

16 *Eweida v. British Airways* (2010) EWCA civ 80, para 37.

religious tolerance, the news media and respect for the theist

introduction

We have from time to time heard calls for greater tolerance to be shown to atheism. This is justified on the grounds of freedom of expression and speech. But it may be that the greatest threat to freedom of belief is not to the atheist or the agnostic; rather it is to the believer in God, whether they be Christian or Muslim. Sometimes it seems as though religion in general, and Christianity in particular, is under attack in the supposedly Christian West,[1] where secularism appears to reign supreme.[2] Though atheists and agnostics are often also proponents of secularism, secularism is not the same as either atheism or agnosticism.[3] We are told that religious intolerance causes wars, and so, by extension, religious belief, and religion itself are attacked. These attacks appear to be led by an alliance (presumably unconscious rather than planned) of liberal elements in the media and of social reformers in other positions of influence. If the suggestion that religion is under attack seems exaggerated, let us examine some of the evidence. The case study we shall use is the Muhammad cartoons controversy, and the reaction of the news media to it.

the Muhammad cartoons and freedom of expression and religion

The publication in the West and elsewhere in 2005 of the so-called Muhammad cartoons, originally printed in the Danish newspaper *Jyllands-Posten*, raised a number of important – and difficult – questions.[4] These went far beyond freedom of speech, which seemed to be the immediate justification for the republication of these cartoons in Western newspapers. Most of the issues which the controversy highlighted remain with us.

In September 2005, as part of an editorial on self-censorship and Islam, *Jyllands-Posten* published twelve cartoons depicting the Prophet Muhammad. The images and representation were not flattering.

The *Qur'an* does not absolutely prohibit the depiction of the Prophet Muhammad.[5] There is an understanding both under Shari'a, and in Islam generally, that depictions of the Prophet are prohibited. However, there is no explicit Sura in the Qur'an that prohibits the creation or use of imagery of the Prophet. There is a long tradition under Shari'a of prohibiting these images. The source of this prohibition can be traced back to the prohibition on idolatry that is discussed in the Qur'an. Sura 42:11 states:

> (He is) the Creator Of the heavens and The earth: He has made For you pairs From among yourselves, And pairs among cattle: By this means does He Multiply you: there is nothing whatever like unto Him, and He is the One that hears and sees (all things).

Many Muslims read this particular Sura as not permitting a human attempt to recreate Allah because there is "nothing whatever like unto Him".

However, many Muslims tolerate some form of depiction, and only some condemn pictorial representations of any kind.[6] It was the satirical intent of the 2005 cartoonists, and the association of the Prophet with terrorism, that was offensive to a large number of Muslims.[7] Disrespect to Islam or to the Prophet Muhammad is still widely considered by Muslims to be blasphemous or sacrilegious. Islamic opinion did not generally maintain that the Western media could not depict the Prophet Muhammad, but that they should not do so in an offensive or disrespectful manner. It could be argued that the right of freedom of thought and expression cannot imply the right to offend the religious sentiments of believers.[8] However, neither can these sentiments be an excuse for calls to "massacre those who insult Islam", as we saw on Muslim protestors' banners in London and elsewhere in 2005.[9]

The problem is more specific than a clash of religions or cultures. It is the attitude of the West reflected in its news media. Typical of this attitude is the editorial statement in the *New Zealand Herald* at the time of the Mohammed cartoon controversy, that "the press is free to give religious offence if it wishes". Legally this may be true, for like the United Kingdom, and unlike large parts of the world, in New Zealand there is a free and independent press, subject only to certain limited restraints covered by defamation and censorship laws.

However, does the media have the moral or ethical right (without assuming that there is necessarily a distinction between morality and ethics) to publish material that they know is offensive to a significant body of people, and particularly where they know that the publication of this is liable, indeed likely, to have serious social, political or other repercussions? The answer, at least according to many in the media, appears to be yes. This suggests that rather than being tolerant of religious beliefs, they use freedom of expression and of the press as a justification for demeaning the beliefs of religious peoples. One might be tolerant of religious belief and yet demean it, but to demean a belief system is unlikely to generate tolerance.

There is also the question of whether Islamic prohibitions – such as they are, for opinion is divided on precisely what is allowed – on the depiction of the Prophet Muhammad can, or ought to, be imposed (legally or otherwise) outside Islamic countries. Perhaps they should not. This can be seen in the other side of tolerance – the believer against the non-believer. However, is it wise, or right, to argue for the right to publish pictures that we know will cause offense, and which may have serious political or economic consequences? It could perhaps be seen as cowardice to say, "don't publish", for these reasons alone. But Christians are taught by Jesus to treat others as we would wish to be treated ourselves. The right of free speech has always been subject to reasonable limitations.[10] One of these, though it may not be enunciated in law, should be the need to avoid deliberate and undue offence and hurt – for to do otherwise is to be intolerant of belief. Self-interest must, however, also play a part.

To publish such cartoons played into the hands of the extremists and undermined the position of many Muslims around the world, when they saw the Western media apparently deliberately attacking Islam. We encourage militants when we act in a way that can be seen as provocative. There was little Western governments could do except hope that their news media would be cautious and prudent, but to the more extreme elements of Islam such niceties might not be apparent.

We know that the actions of some elements of the news media cannot be used to condemn whole countries – or indeed the West as a whole (there was no move to attack Jordan for the publication of the cartoons by a newspaper there, but then Jordan is an Islamic country). Denmark, and the other countries that were the subject of Muslim anger, are Christian – or at least ostensibly so. This controversy tended to polarise attitudes, and widen pre-existing divides. The news media showed intolerance, or at least poor judgment, insensitivity or arrogance, in insisting on their right to cause offence.

religious tolerance and the Western news media

We return to the key moral question: whether the news media is free to give religious offence if it wishes to do so, and whether a decision to do so shows a deliberate policy to attack religious beliefs.

Clearly the news media has, in fact, given offence many times in the past, and will doubtless continue to do so in the future. They have published pictures which have been highly offensive to Christians, but have generally managed to justify their actions (or at least avoid serious legal consequences) on the grounds of freedom of the press. This concept has become so entrenched in the West that we don't look beyond the bland assertion of 'free speech'. Nevertheless, with freedom comes responsibility.[11] Most of the news media is aware of this, but regretfully not all elements are always as scrupulous as they might be to exercise their freedom responsibly. We should ask why these elements of the news media have chosen to "publish and be damned".[12] Is it because they genuinely believe that "the press is free to give religious offence if it wishes", or is it that they wish to attack religious beliefs in particular?

At a time when the Christian roots of Western civilisation are under attack in the West we fail to perceive that many in the non-Christian world, and especially the Islamic world, see us differently from how we see ourselves. To many in the Islamic world the Christian West both fears Islam and is hostile to it. The irony that many, if not most, people in the West are neither Christian nor care whether offence is felt by Christians or Muslims, so long as their comfortable lives are not affected, may escape them. Worse, that very dominance of secularity is likely to further fuel Islamic contempt for the secular (atheist or neo-pagan) West. It has been suggested that modern Christian inclusivity and tolerance is less tolerant than was anciently the case,[13] but whether this is correct or not, the perception of the Christian as being marginalised in a predominantly secular culture may serve to heighten the real or perceived differences between the Christian and the atheist or agnostic population, and likewise the perceived or real inflexibility of the Christian in the face of opposition from their "natural" allies.

No longer predominantly Christian, the West has adopted a secular ideology of freedom which now seems to assert that nothing is sacrosanct, nothing immune from attack,[14] and for that reason alone, to some people, Christianity and Islam ought to be the target of attacks.[15] It is little wonder that many in Islamic societies see the West as decadent and corrupt.[16]

To the Islamic commentators who asked whether we would accept offensive depictions of Christ, we would answer yes, as we have done in the not so distant past – and continue to do.[17] That is not to say that we have been right to do so. Freedom of speech may have gone too far when we can stand back and attempt to justify offensive depictions of the Prophet Muhammad, or condone offensive depictions of religious figures of our own majority religion.

Does this mean that the forces of political correctness should prevail, and that we should impose censorship for fear of offending religious groups – though strangely there seems to have been little inclination to do so when Christianity was the target? It is arguable that the answer should be no.

The news media, and anyone in a position to influence opinion for good or ill, should exercise judgment based on the ideals of decency and good taste, as well as freedom of the press and of speech. The desire to raise readership (or viewer) figures by offending certain groups (Christian or Muslim) who are seen as 'soft targets' should be avoided. There is no excuse for gratuitous insults of any belief or group. Equally, the temptation to assign guilt for the actions of a few individuals to entire religions, cultures or countries should be resisted, whether we are considering offensive cartoons, wars or terrorism. Tolerance of religious views ought to include tolerance for the believer in God just as much as for the non-believer. Legislation throughout the Western world would generally provide for freedom of religion – but seems more effective in protecting the atheist than the theist.

For us in the West, the question must be broader than simply how we show tolerance of the religious beliefs of people and communities – it goes to the core of how we see ourselves. One aspect of twenty-first century culture which is most remarkable is the intellectual dominance of secularism. Society is undergoing, in the West at least, a rapid and seemingly irreversible secularisation. This evolution has not been without its effects on the constitutions of states, despite the oft-quoted (though not necessarily very accurate) principle of the separation of church and state.[18] A state is not without some elements of an ethos, or an underlying philosophical or moral identity.

But a widespread disillusionment with liberal democratic or communist models of government, with capitalism and socialism, and with materialism in its many forms, has left the state, in many societies, unable to provide the degree of conceptual unity of focus which it might be expected to. This has been exacerbated by declining homogeneity and increased political, social, cultural, and economic polarisation and marginalisation. Prior to the nineteenth century Christianity was dominant in the West, so the focus of religious tolerance laws was minority Christian denominations. The beneficiaries were assumed to be theists. Now, although law still assumes this, there is greater emphasis on freedom of expression. This is coupled with an apparent belief that theists are 'fair game'. It is assumed that Christians are unwilling actively to defend their beliefs – but it is a mistake to assume this of Islam also.

Increased diversity in a pluralist society is said to bring strength, but it perhaps cannot do so if it means there is little or no sense of common identity or unity in the state.[19] Iraq, which is riven by religious and ethnic division, is a case in point. Only when diversity becomes the underlying principle of the state – as arguably it has in several countries including the United Kingdom and the United States of America – can it strengthen the state, rather than weaken it. This is because the state which enjoins diversity, applauds difference, is not riven by differences; rather it welcomes this. But even in those countries which do celebrate difference and diversity it is unclear that this actually leads to greater social cohesion.

All is not yet lost. Even those polls that suggest that the majority of people in the United Kingdom don't believe in God also show that a larger proportion of the population regards Christmas as a Christian festival, and want the religious element preserved. This is also true of the Christian elements of state life – the title of the Sovereign as Defender of the Faith, and her or his constitutional role in the Church of England (and even in the Presbyterian Church of Scotland), are generally approved as socially beneficial. Most polls actually suggest that a majority of people do believe in God, even if they have rather unformed views as to who God may be. Fortunately we are still able, in the United Kingdom, to wish someone a 'merry Christmas' without fear of prosecution for causing religious offence. Long may that continue. Religious tolerance must include tolerance for religious believers of both Christian and non-Christian persuasions.

conclusion

Attacks on religious belief, justified on the basis of freedom of speech or of expression, are a challenge to organised religions. Islam and Christianity alike are subject to attacks which appear inspired more by a desire to cause offense, or to 'test the boundaries' of what is acceptable, than by any desire to promote informed debate. This situation, if true, presents a potentially serious threat to the freedom of belief of the theist.

references

1   Contrary to Locke: John Locke, *A Letter Concerning Toleration*, (ed.) Tom Crawford (New York: Dover Thrift, 2002) (1689), p. 145.

2   See Stephen Mansfield, *Ten Tortured Words: How the Founding Fathers Tried to Protect Religion in America and What's Happened Since* (New York: Thomas Nelson, 2007).

3   See Henri Pena-Ruiz, *Histoire de la laïcité: Genèse d'un idéal* (Gallimard: collection Découvertes, 2005).

4   See Flemming Rose, 'Muhammedsansigt' [The Face of Mohammed], *Jyllands-Postenn* (Denmark), (30 September 2005), reprinted in Anders Jerikow and Mille Rode (eds.), *Profet-Affaeren [The Prophet Affair]* (Copenhagen: Dansk PEN, 2006), pp. 14-15.

5   Stéphanie Lagoutte, 'The cartoon controversy in context: Analyzing the decision not to prosecute under Danish law', *Brooklyn Journal of International Law*, 33(2008) pp. 379-403, at p. 389.

6   In art, for instance, the staunch attitude of most jurists is often infringed. See Titus Burkhardt, *Art of Islam: Language and Meaning* (London: World of Islam Festival Publishing Co. Ltd, 1976), p. 33.

7   Rachel Saloom, 'You dropped a bomb on me, Denmark – A legal examination of the cartoon controversy and response as it relates to the Prophet Muhammad and Islamic law', *Rutgers Journal of Law and Religion*, 8 (Fall 2006), pp. 1-37.

8   The origins of freedom of religion can be traced in John C. Laursen and Cary J. Nederman (eds.), *Beyond the Persecuting Society. Religious Toleration Before the Enlightenment* (Philadelphia, PA: University of Pennsylvania Press, 1998); Perez Zagorin, *How the Idea of Religious Toleration Came to the West* (Princeton, NJ: Princeton University Press, 2003). See also Nicholas P. Miller, 'The dawn of the age of toleration: Samuel Pufendorf and the road not taken', *Journal of Church and State*, 50/2 (Spring 2008) pp. 255-276.

9   For the legal context of the cartoons, see Niraj Nathwani, 'Religious cartoons and human rights – A critical legal analysis of the case law of the European Court of Human Rights on the protection of religious feelings and its implications on the Danish affair concerning cartoons of the Prophet Muhammad', *European Human Rights Law Review*, 4 (2008) pp. 488-507.

10 Peter G. Danchin, 'Of Prophets and proselytes: Freedom of religion and the conflict of rights in international law', *Harvard International Law Journal*, 49 (2008) pp. 249-321.

11 John Stuart Mill, *On Liberty* (4th edn, London: Longman, Roberts & Green, 1869).

12 Attributed to Arthur Wellesley, Duke of Wellington, when the courtesan Harriette Wilson threatened to publish her memoirs and his letters.

13 Thomas C. Oden, *The Rebirth of Orthodoxy: Signs of New Life in Christianity* (New York: Harper San Francisco, 2003) p. 115.

14 Ironically, in contrast to this the duty of a Christian priest is to communicate Christian teaching in a "tolerant and gentle" yet disciplined way (2 Tim 2:23ff).

15   For examples of militant atheism, see Christopher Hitchens, *God is not Great: How Religion Poisons Everything* (Crows Nest, N.S.W.: Allen & Unwin, 2007); Richard Dawkins, *The God Delusion* (Boston: Houghton Mifflin Co., 2006).

16   Policy Exchange, 'Living Apart Together:British Muslims and the paradox of multiculturalism', www.policyexchange.org.uk/publications.aspx?id=307

17   See, for instance, *Piss Christ*, which was a controversial photograph by American photographer Andres Serrano. It depicted a small plastic crucifix submerged in a glass of the artist's urine. The piece was a winner of the Southeastern Centre for Contemporary Art's 'Awards in the Visual Arts' competition.

18   See Noel Cox, *Church and State in the Post-Colonial Era: The Anglican Church and the Constitution in New Zealand* (Auckland: Polygraphia, 2008).

19   Allan Rosas, Jan Helgesen and Diane Goodman (eds.), *The Strength of Diversity: Human Rights and Pluralist Democracy* (Leiden: Brill, 1992).

God in the courtroom

The year 2011 ended with a call in the Scottish press for the abolition of the religious oath in Scots courts. An advocate[1] at the Scottish Bar wrote to *The Herald* rguing that it was time to "reconsider the place of religion in the legal process." The correspondent noted two purposes to the oath: that the witness is promising to be truthful and shall answer to God if they are not; and that there is a change to their status from that of an 'everyday citizen' to a person who must answer questions truthfully to avoid committing an offence.[2]

Noting the changing religious landscape in Scotland since the alternative affirmation[3] was introduced more than 200 years ago, the author considered the oath to be "anachronistic". His difficulty with the religious oath was essentially one of perception:

> The problem with affirmation is that it sets a witness out and it instantly draws a great deal of attention to the fact that the person will not swear to God. It is a statement relating to a person's personality and belief that no other witness is required to make, unless it is a facet of the particular case. It is impossible to be certain that such an aspect of the witnesses' personality will not affect the views of some jurors as to the quality of their evidence. Those holding extremely strong (potentially bigoted) religious views may dismiss everything the witness says in light of their affirmation. Even if the juror is not that strongly affected, but still affected to a degree, then there is potential for an unfair verdict that need not exist in a modern legal system.

The learned correspondent's contention was that God has no place in the Scottish court, for fear (principally) that a juror, being the fact-finder in such trials, might somehow think less of a witness' evidence if he has affirmed, and thereby simply sworn by himself. The solution, the author argued, was for there to be a "single oath for everyone regardless of belief or religion."

The letter drew a rapid response from other correspondents who argued that not only was the religious oath anachronistic but that it was, in fact, "positively unChristian", citing Jesus' well known injunction in the Sermon on the Mount:

Again you have heard that it was said to those of old, 'You shall not swear falsely, but shall perform to the Lord what you have sworn.' But I say to you, Do not take an oath at all, either by heaven, for it is the throne of God, or by the earth, for it is his footstool, or by Jerusalem, for it is the city of the great King. And do not take an oath by your head, for you cannot make one hair white or black. Let what you say simply be 'Yes' or 'No'; anything more than this comes from evil.[4]

Broader reaction was mixed. One of Scotland's best known QCs rejected the suggestion that juries may be swayed by the way in which a witness did or did not swear, but identified the problem that "many who don't believe in God start their court experience with a lie."[5] Another legal figure argued that the weakness of a single oath was that "you have to swear on something otherwise it [the oath] is meaningless."[6] A Church of Scotland spokesman also rejected the proposal, observing:

For people of faith the upholding of justice begins with God, not just the law of the land. When called to serve their neighbour by giving evidence, people of faith should be allowed to reflect their beliefs in the manner in which they make their vows in the same way as those who don't believe in God should be able to choose a vow that reflects their beliefs.[7]

This paper will examine the current law in Scotland and will then seek to answer the vexed question of whether oaths are, in fact, 'unChristian', before briefly considering the position from the perspective of another religion, Islam. Finally, and in light of this analysis, the place of the Christian oath in the Scottish court will be considered.

the current law

At present in Scotland, all witnesses, other than children and the mentally incapable, must take the oath before they give evidence.[8] The practice is governed by the Oaths Act 1978. In the terms of this legislation, the oath is equally binding on the person who has taken it, even if that person has no religious belief.[9] Such a person, if he or she objects to taking a religious oath, can instead make a solemn affirmation.[10] The current form of the religious oath in Scotland is "I swear by Almighty God that I will tell the truth, the whole truth, and nothing but the truth."[11] The form of affirmation is "I solemnly, sincerely and truly declare and affirm that I will tell the truth, the whole truth, and nothing but the truth." Regardless of whether an oath or affirmation has been taken, the force of these is considered to be the same in law, and a witness who lies having sworn or affirmed is equally liable for prosecution for perjury if he or she fails to tell the truth in evidence.

the theological position

Is swearing by God contrary to scripture? A simplistic reading of Jesus' words might lead to that conclusion, but a deeper understanding of the problem Jesus was addressing is required before a final view can be properly formed.

References to swearing oaths are common in the Old Testament. Space does not permit a full examination of them here. What is clear, though, is that the taking of oaths was in no way prohibited by the Old Testament – indeed, specific provision was made for it.

Moses told the people of Israel "It is the Lord your God you shall fear. Him you shall serve and by his name you shall swear."[12] Elsewhere, provision was made in the law for the taking of an oath to have probative effect. For example, in Exodus 22.10-11, dealing with disputes arising from the death or loss of an animal in the care of the owner's neighbour, the owner would be required to accept the keeper's oath taken before God that he was not responsible. This had such force because, as one commentator observed, the keeper in swearing an oath was "invoking a curse upon himself…if he did not tell the truth God would make the curse effective."[13]

If that is the case, what was the difficulty by the time Jesus gave the apparent injunction? The cultural situation into which he was speaking is succinctly summarised by a commentator in the following way:

> To protect the sanctity of the divine name against inadvertent oath-breaking, common Jewish practice introduced surrogate objects by which to swear…Some people apparently thought it harmless to deceive if they swore by something like their right hand…The further removed the oath was from the actual name of God, the less danger they faced for violating it.[14]

So was the issue in the culture the taking of oaths *per se* or was it the cheapening of truth? The practice that had developed recognised that swearing by God's name was serious, but there was a view that swearing by 'lesser' things was less binding – something like the modern equivalent of a person telling a lie with his fingers crossed behind his back.

If, therefore, the issue was the abuse of oaths, and the creation of artificial layers of truthfulness, was Jesus actually prohibiting the taking of an oath?

The key message Jesus was conveying, it is submitted, was to be truthful at all times, regardless of the context, or any legal ceremonies that had been gone through. This is clear from Matthew 5.37 – truthfulness should be central to our speech, irrespective of the context.

So does Jesus teach that it is wrong to take any oath at all? My contention is no. As others assert, such a proposition is not in accordance with the teaching of the Bible as a whole.[15] Indeed, Jesus himself later allowed himself to be put on oath before confirming himself to be the Christ, and later scriptural references confirm the practice of oath taking without criticism.[16] The issue, rather, "is the condemnation of the flippant, profane, uncalled for, and often hypocritical oath, used in order to make an impression."[17] In light of all of this, can a Christian take an oath before God? There is no theological reason not to.

The essence of any criminal trial is ultimately to resolve a factual dispute, and within the (largely) adversarial Scottish system, the prosecution seeks to prove that which it alleges in the indictment predominantly on the basis of oral evidence. Anyone with experience of the criminal courts can testify that lies are all too often told by some (though by no means all) witnesses. The reasons for this are varied. The barrister and author John Munkman identified two broad categories of untruthful witnesses: the "deliberate liar" and "the witness who, while taking great care to speak the literal truth, is yet keeping something back."[18]

Getting to the truth is essential to resolve the factual dispute in a criminal trial. The Old Testament context of dispute resolution prescribed severe consequences of being untruthful in evidence. While in the modern era public prosecutions are the norm (indeed in Scotland private prosecutions are virtually unheard of), in Old Testament times the system of prosecution was private, with the victim or accuser being the "personal enemy of the accused, who might be acting with malicious intent."[19] Where the dispute was so personal and the stakes were high, the punishment for lying was severe: in Deuteronomy 19.19-21 the malicious witness would bear the punishment that he intended for the accused. As David McIlroy points out, "Lying about someone else's involvement in a crime was to be treated as morally equivalent to committing the crime itself."[20]

The witness is thus, in a sense, on trial himself when giving evidence, in that if his evidence is in any way contentious, one side in the adversarial system will be trying to present him as being mistaken (at best) or (at worst) a liar. How can a witness emphasise his truthfulness? On what can he call? Here the need is clear for some way of accentuating both the requirement of truthfulness, and something to which the truthful witness can pray in aid of his integrity. As one commentator has pointed out, "in this world of dishonesty and deception the oath is at times necessary to add solemnity and the guarantee of reliability to an important affirmation or promise."[21]

As was considered above in the context of Old Testament dispute resolution, the person taking the oath was essentially invoking a curse upon himself should he lie. While an oath may be administered by a secular judge in a secular court, it is intrinsically a matter between the taker of the oath and God. Jesus said we should be truthful always, but it may be seen that to invoke God's name and then lie could bring considerable dishonour to that name. For a Christian believer, the issue and consequences could hardly be more serious.

The oath, therefore, is not intrinsically wrong. Rather, what was to be abhorred then (as now) was its misuse, or any legalistic formulation to somehow lessen its impact. At root, the emphasis should always be on the truthfulness of the words spoken in evidence, not the precise formulation preceding them.

a comparison from Islam

If the Christian is not, therefore, prohibited from taking the oath, but is neither under obligation to take it, on the basis he should at all times be truthful, is the position the same for a Muslim?

Commentators on Islamic law argue that "[o]aths, or the refusal to swear an oath, can have probative force."[22] The reason for this is that Islamic law

> is a religious system of law, and it is understood that those who come before the court will mostly be Muslims who will have a belief in God and a belief that they risk severe punishment in the hereafter if they lie on oath.[23]

Hajj Ahmad Thomson, a practising barrister and a Muslim, citing a number of passages from the Qur'an, concludes that:

> In a court of law a Muslim should always swear "by Allah" that he or she is going to tell the truth. If a Muslim avoids doing so, either by refusing to swear an oath at all or by electing to make some other form of oath such as an oath of affirmation, it can safely be inferred from this that he or she either fears or knows that he or she will not be telling the whole truth.[24]

If there is an argument that a Muslim should swear an oath, an inference might therefore be drawn from a refusal to do so. But while such inference, as Thomson points out, cannot always be that the witness intends to lie, it may add some weight to the original view cited at the start of this paper that jurors might question the witness' evidence.

That recognised, the faith (or lack thereof) of an affirming witness may not be immediately apparent to a court, and in the absence of such knowledge, it is hard to see how a juror would be able to form a view on a decision to affirm. Moreover, even if a witness' faith was apparent (for example by his mode of dress), whether any given juror (of any faith or none) would have a sufficient understanding of the relevant theological intricacies is questionable, perhaps reducing the risk of an adverse inference being drawn.

proposals for reform

If nothing else, a brief look into the history of this area confirms that "there is nothing new under the sun."[25] Indeed, proposals to abolish the oath have been mooted since the days of Jeremy Bentham.[26] The matter was considered at some length by the Thomson Committee in Scotland in the 1970s, whose report significantly shaped changes in criminal procedure thereafter.[27] The Committee sought the view of the Church of Scotland and the Roman Catholic Church. Both supported the retention of the religious aspect of the oath.[28] The Church of Scotland acknowledged an oath could not make a witness truthful, but cited evidence from their Panel of Doctrine that the oath "is a decided deterrent, and certainly makes a witness realise that he must tell the truth."[29] The Catholic Church too considered the oath to be "a strong deterrent to the giving of false testimony."[30] Ultimately, the committee, whilst acknowledging the truism that the taking of an oath cannot prevent witnesses from telling lies, did not dissent from the view that "the taking of the oath prevents some witnesses from telling lies."[31]

The matter was later considered by Iain Macphail in 1987.[32] While acknowledging the strong arguments for the abolition of the religious oath, he agreed that it should not be abolished unless something "more meaningful, more generally acceptable and more likely to serve the cause of justice" could be found.[33] Ultimately Macphail considered that while the oath is regularly dishonoured, it does serve

> to bring home most strongly the solemnity of [the witness'] obligation to tell the truth and to give their evidence with care. It may be thought that any proposal to abolish the oath in Scottish proceedings would be likely to cause widespread misunderstanding and offence. In any event it would probably be difficult to secure general agreement on the wording of any new declaration.[34]

The logic of this conclusion is hard to criticise. The oath may be imperfect. It may often be perfunctory, at least in the minds of many witnesses who swear it. It even might create a reaction in the eyes of the occasional juror. But whether any alternative system would truly be better is, at best, debatable.

closing thoughts

There can be no doubt that, as the *Herald's* correspondent asserted, the religious landscape in Scotland has changed dramatically in the last two decades, let alone the last two centuries. While the Church of Scotland remains the national Church, some suggest that at its current rate of decline it may not exist beyond the 2030s.[35]

Whatever transpires, in noting that no one would ever be compelled to swear before God in court against their will, the question is whether there fundamentally remains a place for such a Christian act or declaration in the secular context of a criminal trial.

From the perspective of the lawful requirement to tell the truth in evidence, whether the witness swears or affirms is essentially irrelevant. While a person of faith should be free to swear an oath in a form appropriate to their belief, there is a compelling argument that such a decision should always be respected as a personal and private matter of faith.

The witness who desires to swear, be he a committed, Bible-believing Christian, or otherwise someone who in some way would (to a greater or lesser extent) identify himself as a Christian, is operating within a secular trial where his truthfulness and integrity is being put to the test. That witness may, and should, be permitted to call God as a witness to the truthfulness of his evidence.

To do so is entirely permissible and proper under God. It is doubtful that jurors would genuinely be swayed negatively by someone taking an oath, any more than that they would think less of a witness who chose to affirm. But, taking that issue aside, in any event, as an act of religious freedom and tolerance, to remove the ability of the Christian to swear in order to accentuate the truthfulness of his evidence would be to deny part of his character – which in one sense is what is being tested in evidence.

The author is grateful to Dr David McIlroy for his helpful comments on a draft of this paper. Any views expressed in this paper, together with any errors, inaccuracies or omissions are, of course, my own.

references

1   The Scottish equivalent of a barrister.

2   Letters, *The Herald* (26 December 2011).

3   To affirm is "to declare solemnly as a witness to the truth of one's evidence when one objects to taking an oath." The Law Society of Scotland, Glossary – Scottish Legal Terms, Latin Maxims and European Community Legal Terms (Butterworths,1988), p. 8.

4   Letters, *The Herald* (27 December 2011). See also: Letters, (29 December 2011). The text is Matthew 5.33-35. All biblical quotations are taken from the English Standard Version.

5   'Top QC calls for abolition of religious oath in court', *The Herald* (26 December 2011).

6   Ibid.

7   Ibid.

8   Walker & Walker, *The Law of Evidence in Scotland* (Tottel Publishing, 2009) 3rd edition p. 215.

9   Oaths Act 1978, section 4(2).

10 Ibid., section 5(1).

11 *The Law of Evidence in Scotland*, p. 216.

12 Deuteronomy 6.13.

13 G.C.D. Howley & Others, *A Bible Commentary for Today* (Pickering & Inglis Ltd, 1979) p. 195.

14 IVP New Testament Commentaries, Matthew, 'Oaths Are a Poor Substitute for Integrity', available at http://www.biblegateway.com/resources/commentaries/IVP-NT/Matt/Oaths-Poor-Substitute.

15 William Hendriksen, *New Testament Commentary, The Gospel of Matthew*, (The Banner of Truth Trust, 1973) p. 309.

16 Ibid. See, for example 2 Corinthians 1.23 where the Apostle Paul called God as his witness. See also Hebrews 6.16.

17 Ibid.

18 John H. Munkman, *The Technique of Advocacy* (Universal Law Publishing Co. Pvt. Ltd., 1951, 2007 Reprint) p. 33.

19 Christopher D. Marshall, *Beyond Retribution* (Eerdmans Publishing Company, 2001) p. 48.

20 David McIlroy, *A Biblical View of Law and Justice* (Paternoster Press, 2004) p. 86.

21 Hendriksen, *New Testament Commentary*, op. cit. p. 309.

22 Lawrence Rosen, *The Justice of Islam* (Oxford: Oxford University Press, 2000) p. 12. Note however, as Rosen observes, that for some more serious crimes, a defendant's refusal to swear an oath is not probative (p. 13).

23 Jamila Hussain, *Islamic Law and Society, An Introduction* (The Federation Press, 1999) p. 156.

24 Hajj Ahmad Thomson, 'The significance for a Muslim of swearing or refusing to swear an oath on the Qur'an,' Available at http://www.wynnechambers.co.uk/pdf/Swearing_an_Oath.pdf p. 8, though Thomson earlier acknowledges that the reason for any unwillingness on the part

of a Muslim to swear an oath may be based on an uncertainty as to the truth, rather than an unwillingness to tell it (p. 7).

25   Ecclesiastes 1.9.

26   I.D. Macphail, *Evidence* (The Law Society of Scotland, Butterworths, 1987), para 8.05.

27   'Criminal Procedure in Scotland' (Second Report), Cmnd. 6218.

28   Ibid., at paras 42.08 – 42.10.

29   Ibid., at para 42.09.

30   Ibid., at para 42.10(b).

31   Ibid., at para 42.11.

32   A Sheriff and then, from 2005 until his death in 2009 a Senator of the College of Justice (a High Court Judge in Scotland).

33   *Evidence*, op. cit. para 8.07.

34   Ibid.

35   Stuart Murray, *Post-Christendom* (Paternoster Press, 2004) p. 6.

Westminster and Strasbourg: an uneasy relationship?

introduction

Though a principal result of the Human Rights Act 1998 has been that claimants can now plead alleged breaches of the European Convention of Human Rights (ECHR) in the courts of the United Kingdom, it still remains possible to appeal to the European Court of Human Rights (ECtHR) in Strasbourg. The proviso is that one must first exhaust the available domestic remedies – but the process of exhaustion may not necessarily involve a prior appeal to the Supreme Court. Claims based on the Convention have become more common since 1998, as claimants and their advisers have become more aware of its provisions.

Far from heralding this as an advance, however, on this side of the Channel much of the press reaction to the Convention and the Court has been extremely hostile. "Europe's war on British justice: UK loses three out of four human rights cases", trumpeted the *Daily Mail* in January 2012 or, somewhat less hysterically, "Let Parliament rule on our human rights", said *The Daily Telegraph* in March. "Strasbourg-bashing", said Supreme Court Justice Lady Hale in a recent lecture, "has become very popular."[1]

The problem centres around two issues: the degree to which the ECtHR is prepared to concede that the domestic courts are sometimes in a better position than Strasbourg to judge what is appropriate in local circumstances – in the jargon, the 'margin of appreciation' – and the extent to which the Council of Europe collectively, as guardian of the Convention, is prepared to leave decision-making on the application of the Convention to domestic governments and parliaments – the principle of 'subsidiarity'.

The general feeling of unease that Strasbourg is too interventionist has led to widespread calls for change. One of the most vociferous critics, Daniel Hannan, a Conservative MEP and currently Secretary-General of the Alliance of European Conservatives and Reformists in the European Parliament, has argued, in effect, for withdrawal from the Convention. "Most politicians," he suggests, "together with virtually the entire legal establishment, take our continued membership as a *datum* or given; yet they rarely get round to explaining why it's so necessary"[2] – to which his response is that it is *not* necessary and its supposed benefits are almost entirely illusory.

Nor are such misgivings limited to the usual suspects on the Centre-Right. When the House of Commons voted in 2011 for a continued ban on prisoners voting in elections in defiance of the ruling of the Grand Chamber of the European Court of Human Rights in *Hirst*,[3] the motion to endorse the ban was in the names of David Davis and Jack Straw: a former Conservative Party Chairman in cahoots with a former Labour Home Secretary and Lord Chancellor.[4]

Part of the problem is that, traditionally, 'human rights' have been seen as a mechanism for protecting individuals from state oppression whereas, in reality, the reach of the Convention has moved far beyond that. Or as the newest member of the Supreme Court, Lord Sumption, put it in a recent lecture:

> [O]ne of the great unspoken problems about human rights law…is that very many human rights issues are in reality not issues between the state and its citizens. They are issues between different groups of citizens, whose resolution by democratic processes will not necessarily lead to the same answer everywhere.[5]

The result of this suspicion of the Convention has been a two-pronged assault: a demand for a decisive shift in the balance of power on human rights issues from Strasbourg towards the domestic courts – what one might term 'the repatriation approach' – and calls for more streamlined procedures and a more rigorous filter mechanism to discourage worthless applications to the Strasbourg court – 'the reformist approach'.

Both have been rumbling on for some considerable time. David Cameron raised the issue in 2006 when Leader of the Opposition, arguing for domestic legislation to

> protect the fundamental rights set out in the European Convention…in clearer and more precise terms. Greater clarity and precision would allow those rights to be enforced more easily and effectively in circumstances where they ought to be protected but it would become harder to extend them inappropriately as under the present law.[6]

Jack Straw then took up the theme in a lecture in 2007. He dismissed the suggestion that simply repealing the Human Rights Act 1988 and enacting a new domestic Bill of Rights in its place would lead to a greater margin of appreciation in Strasbourg. However, he suggested that there was a danger that rights "become commoditised, yet more items to be 'claimed'…in a selfish way without regard to others",[7] and said that he would be working with the Review of Citizenship being conducted by the former Attorney General, Lord

Goldsmith, to look at how a British Bill of Rights and Responsibilities might help to foster a stronger sense of citizenship by establishing and articulating the balance between rights and obligations.

Fast forward to March 2011, when the Cameron Government established an independent Commission on a Bill of Rights to investigate the creation of a UK Bill of Rights that incorporates and builds on all our obligations under the European Convention on Human Rights, ensures that these rights continue to be enshrined in UK law, and protects and extends our liberties.[8]

The Commission published interim advice to ministers in advance of the United Kingdom's assuming the Chair of the Council of Europe, recommending that the Government should vigorously pursue urgent and fundamental reform of the Court to ensure that it addressed only those cases "that raise serious questions affecting the interpretation or application of the Convention and serious issues of general importance", and use its Chairmanship to that end.[9]

The interim advice and a follow-up letter from the Commission's Chairman, Sir Leigh Lewis, were insufficiently robust for one of the Commissioners, Dr Michael Pinto-Duschinsky, who resigned in March 2012 and told the BBC's *Sunday Politics* programme on 12 March that "the Commission has been consistently directed by the Chairman…away from consideration of parliamentary override", and that "it's been intended all along to issue a report in favour of the *status quo*."[10]

Few would go so far as Hannan and argue for total withdrawal from the Convention: certainly not Pinto-Duschinsky himself, who put on record in *The Guardian* that he was not seeking "to abandon the rights set out in the ECHR. A British bill of rights would be 'ECHR plus'"[11]; nor the present Government, which confirmed as recently as May 2012 that "we have no plans to leave the Convention".[12] Moreover, withdrawing from the Convention would almost certainly trigger the Armageddon of forced withdrawal from the European *Union*, since the EU Charter of Fundamental Rights, in effect, incorporates the Convention into EU law by affirming in its Preamble, *inter alia*, "the European Convention for the Protection of Human Rights and Fundamental Freedoms…and the case-law of the Court of Justice of the European Communities and of the European Court of Human Rights". Similarly, Article 6(2) and (3) of the Treaty of Lisbon provide that the EU "shall accede" to the ECHR and that [f]undamental rights, as guaranteed by the European Convention for the Protection of Human Rights and Fundamental Freedoms and as they result from the constitutional traditions common to the Member States, shall constitute general principles of the Union's law.

Strasbourg and freedom of religion

In spite of this, the issue of Westminster's relationship with Strasbourg clearly continues to niggle with politicians, and one of the most controversial issues has been the perception in some quarters that certain rights are favoured over others, with "the right to freedom of thought, conscience and religion" under Article 9 of the Convention coming fairly low down in the pecking-order.

The more recent high-profile religion cases – *Chaplin* and *Eweida* (both of which involved the wearing of religious symbols while in uniform) and *Ladele* and *McFarlane* (both of which involved objections on religious grounds to providing services for same-sex couples)[13] – have been given extensive media coverage and all four are, at the time of writing, awaiting appeal hearings in Strasbourg. *Ladele* and *McFarlane*, particularly, raise complex issues about the clash of competing rights: the right of same-sex couples to respect for their sexuality under Article 8 ECHR (respect for private and family life) and the right of Ms Ladele and Mr McFarlane to act in accordance with their religious convictions in accordance with Article 9 (freedom of thought, conscience and religion). In September 2011, the Equality and Human Rights Commission submitted an intervention to the Court, arguing that in *Eweida* and *Chaplin* the domestic courts might have given insufficient weight to the qualifications on restriction of religious freedoms in Article 9(2) of the Convention but that in *Ladele* and *McFarlane* the domestic courts had come to the correct conclusions.[14]

It is difficult to see how the wish to wear an inconspicuous cross or crucifix while in uniform could be regarded with the same degree of seriousness as refusing on religious grounds to provide a particular service to same-sex couples, still less that it might engage public safety, public order, health or morals, or even the rights and freedoms of others. The facts in *Eweida* and *Chaplin* look suspiciously like an initial overreaction by the employers followed by dogged persistence for fear of losing face. The issues in *Ladele* and *McFarlane*, on the other hand, are much more fundamental: there were third parties in both cases who were genuinely offended by the religious attitudes of the two claimants and "the rights and freedoms of others" certainly came into account.

But what the four cases are not about is whether or not the manifestation of 'religion' itself is under some kind of Damoclean threat from Strasbourg. However irritating it may be to those who want simple solutions, the fact is that human rights cases of any degree of complexity will almost inevitably involve a clash of rights: for example, the right of Ms Sarikha Watkins-Singh to manifest her Sikhism by wearing a *kara* bangle against the rights of the governors of her school to enforce their policy on school uniform (she won) or the right of Mr Stephen Copsey to observe Sunday as a day of rest in accordance with the

Fourth Commandment against the right of his employers to get the work done that was needed to fulfil their contractual obligations to their customers (he lost).

Watkins-Singh was in some ways a special case, because Sikhs constitute a racial group for the purposes of the race relations legislation and the case was decided on racial grounds rather than religious ones. But there remains a particular problem in relation to the ability of employees to exercise their Article 9 rights to freedom of thought, conscience and religion in the course of their employment. At least since the decision in *Kalaç*[15] in 1997 (which upheld the enforced retirement of a devout Muslim from his position as Director of Legal Affairs of the Turkish Air Force because he was deemed to have adopted "unlawful fundamentalist opinions"), Strasbourg has taken the view that the religious obligations of an employee do not normally take precedence over the operational requirements of his or her employer. In *Kalaç* the ECtHR declared that:

> Article 9 [does] not protect every act motivated or inspired by a religion or belief…
> [I]n exercising his freedom to manifest his religion, an individual may need to take his specific situation into account.[16]

That, in short, is what Russell Sandberg has dubbed "the specific situation rule":[17] more brutally, 'if you don't like it where you work, go and get a job somewhere else'.

It should be said that the courts in the United Kingdom have not always been entirely comfortable either with the rule itself or with its non-interventionist approach to questions of religious manifestation. In *Copsey* Lord Justice Mummery described Strasbourg's approach as "repeated assertions unsupported by the evidence or reasoning that would normally accompany a judicial ruling," and "difficult to square with the supposed fundamental character of the [Article 9] rights".[18] Had it not been for the rulings from Strasbourg he would have found for Mr Copsey but, in the circumstances, he regarded himself as bound by them. Occasional judicial misgivings aside, however, the rule has normally been applied by the domestic courts;[19] and because it limits the degree to which a court can balance the religious sensibilities of the employee with the requirements of the employer, it continues to be a fairly severe restriction on the scope of Article 9. *Chaplin, Eweida, Ladele* and *McFarlane* all engaged the rule to a greater or lesser degree.

A very recent example of its operation is *Doogan*, in which, as a result of a reorganisation, two Roman Catholic midwifery sisters in Glasgow found themselves responsible for supervising and supporting staff caring for patients having abortions.[20] When they complained about the imposed change in their duties and the apparent violation of their rights under Article 9 and attempted to assert their conscientious objection under section 4(1) of the Abortion Act 1967, the judicial rejoinder was that though they might be supervising nurses who were involved in terminations of pregnancy they did not themselves take any part in the actual treatment that procured them – and that they "may need to take [their] specific situation into account".[21] To which they might reasonably have retorted, 'But hang on, that's not what we signed up to in the first place.'

The specific situation rule is problematical; but equally serious, if not more so, is the degree of ignorance (whether real or feigned) around the issue more generally. "Human rights" is bandied around unthinkingly in areas that have nothing whatsoever to do with the Act or the Convention. Like 'health and safety' which – dangerously – have simply become all-purpose boo-words, any reference to 'human rights' tends to evoke instant groans. Perhaps the debate reached its nadir when the Home Secretary told the 2011 Conservative Party Conference about "the illegal immigrant who cannot be deported because, and I am not making this up, he had a pet cat" – and in so saying managed to get both the facts of the case and the judgment completely wrong.[22] Equally dubious was the "UK loses three out of four human rights cases" story in the *Daily Mail*. It is true that between 1966 and the end of 2010 the UK had been found to be in breach of the Convention in 271 cases out of the 443 in which it was a party – but the headline totally ignored the fact that 97 per cent of cases brought against the UK since 1966 had been declared inadmissible or struck out and had never gone to a hearing at all.[23]

How to accommodate conflicting rights is possibly the most difficult issue in human rights law. But what will simply *not* do is to appeal to 'common sense'. Lord Falconer tried that approach in 2007 in a lecture at Manchester Law School delivered while he was Lord Chancellor, asserting that "the law, the Human Rights Act, is common sense. So when they do apply the law, they must then be applying common sense. And coming up with a common sense answer to their human rights problem."[24] Even leaving aside the fact that his argument was circular, its major flaw is that it assumes that the Human Rights Act 1998 *is* 'common sense' – whatever that might be – and that people will always recognise a 'common sense solution' when they see one – whatever *that* might be. And it ducks the killer question: if the law is so certain and so easy to interpret and to apply, how is it that judges ever get overturned on appeal?

so where do we go from here?

From her vantage-point in the Supreme Court Lady Hale sees room for herself and her colleagues

> to develop a distinctively British human rights jurisprudence without overstepping the boundaries which Parliament has set for us. It is just as likely to lead to our respecting the recent judgments of Parliament as it is to our declaring them incompatible.[25]

So far as Strasbourg is concerned, the Council of Europe's High Level Conference on the workings of the Court and the Convention at Brighton in April 2012 may have heralded the beginning of a change in attitudes. It ended with a comprehensive declaration on the operations of the Court which included a statement that "a reference to the principle of subsidiarity and the doctrine of the margin of appreciation as developed in the Court's case law should be included in the Preamble to the Convention."[26] The 2011 judgment in *Lautsi*,[27] in which the Grand Chamber held that the display of crucifixes in the classrooms of state schools was in principle a matter falling within the margin of appreciation of the Italian authorities, may even have signalled a move in that direction.

As to the UK Government's Commission on a Bill of Rights, who knows? A cynic (like me) might wonder why there is thought to be any point in legislating at all if, as Pinto-Duschinsky concedes, a new Act cannot replace or significantly amend the ECHR. But perhaps that is too negative a view; and where new legislation of the right kind might conceivably be of value could be in educating the public on the importance of human rights. It may also be that we are seeing a shift in attitudes both in Strasbourg and at Westminster – although I would still argue that, so long as the United Kingdom is a signatory to the Convention, *the first duty of Government is to do what we have signed up to do*: to respect the Convention and to comply with the judgments of the Court.

The adverse judgment in *Hirst* on the voting rights of prisoners has been largely reaffirmed by Strasbourg in *Scoppola*,[28] a parallel Italian case in which the United Kingdom intervened. The Grand Chamber accepted the Attorney General's argument that each member state had a wide discretion as to how it regulated any ban on votes for prisoners and is prepared to give the United Kingdom a considerable margin of appreciation about the precise way in which it proposes to fulfil the terms of the original judgment. But fulfil the terms of the judgment it must: simply to do nothing is not an option.

How the Government will respond to *Hirst* and *Scoppola* remains to be seen, not least because it will have to persuade a hostile Parliament to pass the necessary legislation – and the immediate reaction of Davis and Straw was: "The Court has ordered us to legislate to give prisoners the vote within six months. We should do no such thing."[29] But a continued refusal of the vote even to those serving very short custodial sentences might look suspiciously like the sacrifice of an international obligation at the altar of the *Daily Mail* – which, predictably, greeted the *Scoppola* judgment with the headline 'Contempt for Our Democracy'.[30]

Leaving aside the prospect of a string of compensation claims from aggrieved prisoners, however, I would contend there is a much more fundamental reason for compliance: that, as a long-established liberal democracy, the United Kingdom is under a compelling moral obligation to uphold human rights domestically in the wider interests of those elsewhere who are massively less fortunate than ourselves. Set against the broader international canvas of serious human rights abuses, wearing a cross with a British Airways uniform or voting rights for convicted prisoners are both very small beer indeed – but how can we criticise countries that routinely commit serious violations of human rights if we are not squeaky-clean ourselves? An uneasy relationship? Emphatically 'yes' – and likely to remain so. Finally, the more explicit coupling of rights' and 'responsibilities' in the way suggested by Jack Straw has its undoubted attractions; but any move in that direction must avoid the trap of implying that the fulfilment of those responsibilities is some kind of measure of whether or not one is a fit and proper member of society. A statutory right to social security benefits does not *necessarily* imply a duty to seek a job, nor does a right to healthcare *necessarily* imply a duty to drink no more than 22 units of alcohol in a week. If rights are sometimes aspirational, duties and responsibilities will also sometimes have to be aspirational: not a series of hoops to jump through but, rather, a series of benchmarks for 'good citizenship'.

references

1   Brenda Hale, 'Argentoratum Locutum: Is Strasbourg or the Supreme Court Supreme?' (2012) Human Rights Law Review 12 (1): pp. 65-78. Her title refers to the three-sentence judgment of the late Lord Rodger of Earlsferry in Secretary of State for the Home Department v AF & Anor [2009] UKHL 28, which concluded, "Even though we are dealing with rights under a United Kingdom statute, in reality, we have no choice: Argentoratum locutum, iudicium finitum – Strasbourg has spoken, the case is closed".

2   'Britain should withdraw from the European Convention on Human Rights', Daily Telegraph Blogs 12 February 2011, http://blogs.telegraph.co.uk/news/danielhannan/100075824/britain-should-withdraw-from-the-european-convention-on-human-rights/ Accessed 22 April 2012.

3   Hirst v United Kingdom (No. 2) 74025/01 [2005] ECHR 681.

4   See Hansard, HC (Series 5) vol. 523, cols 493ff (10 Feb. 2011).

5   Jonathan Sumption, 'Judicial and Political Decision-Making: The Uncertain Boundary', The F. A. Mann Lecture 2011 (Lincoln's Inn, 9 November 2011).

6   David Cameron, 'Balancing freedom and security – a modern British Bill of Rights' (London, 26 June 2006): http://www.britishpoliticalspeech.org/speech-archive.htm?speech=293 Accessed 21 April 2012.

7   Jack Straw, 'Human Rights in the 21st Century': The Mackenzie-Stuart Lecture (Cambridge, 25 October 2007) http://sms.cam.ac.uk/media/1172324 Accessed 21 April 2012.

8   Commission on a Bill of Rights, Discussion Paper: Do we need a UK Bill of Rights? August 2011, para 1.

9   Commission on a Bill of Rights, 'Reform of the European Court of Human Rights: Our Interim Advice to Government,' 8 September 2011, para. 8; http://www.justice.gov.uk/downloads/about/cbr/cbr-court-reform-interim-advice.pdf.

10   Helen Warrell, 'Academic accuses Clarke over bill of rights', Financial Times, 11 March 2012.

11   Michael Pinto-Duschinsky, 'Commission must not compromise by recommending bill identical to HRA' The Guardian, 13 March 2012.

12   During oral questions to the Ministry of Justice: see Hansard, HC (Series 5) col 398 (15 May 2012).

13   Chaplin v Royal Devon and Exeter Hospital NHS Foundation Trust [2010] ET 1702886/2009, Eweida v British Airways Plc [2010] EWCA Civ 80, Ladele v London Borough of Islington [2009] EWCA Civ 1357, McFarlane v Relate Avon Ltd [2010] EWCA Civ B1.

14   Article 9 (2) of the ECHR declares that freedom to manifest "shall be subject only to such limitations as are prescribed by law and are necessary in a democratic society in the interests of public safety, for the protection of public order, health or morals, or the protection of the rights and freedoms of others".

15   Kalaç v Turkey 20704/92 [1997] ECHR 37.

16   Kalaç at para 27.

17 In 'Controversial Recent Claims to Religious Liberty' (2008) *Law Quarterly Review* 124, pp. 213–17 and 'The Changing Position of Religious Minorities in English Law: The Legacy of *Begum*' in R. Grillo et al (eds.) *Legal Practice and Cultural Diversity* (Ashgate, 2009) pp. 267-282.

18 *Copsey v WWB Devon Clays Ltd* [2005] EWCA Civ 932 at paras 35–36.

19 See, for example, Lord Bingham in *Begum, R (on the application of) v Denbigh High School* [2006] UKHL 15 at paras 22–23.

20 *Doogan & Anor, Re Judicial Review* [2012] ScotCS CSOH 32.

21 *Doogan* at para 49, quoting Kalaç.

22 *X v Secretary of State for the Home Department* [2008] Asylum and Immigration Tribunal IA/14578/2008.

23 See Adam Wagner, 'UK loses 3 out of 4 European human rights cases? More like 1 in 50, actually', *UK Human Rights Blog* (12 January 2012) http://ukhumanrightsblog.com/2012/01/12/uk-loses-3-out-of-4-european-human-rights-cases-more-like-1-in-50-actually Accessed 21 April 2012.

24 Lord Falconer, 'Human rights and common sense', *The Harry Street Lecture* (9 February 2007) http://webarchive.nationalarchives.gov.uk/+/http://www.dca.gov.uk/speeches/2007/sp070209.htm Accessed 22 April 2012.

25 *'Argentoratum Locutum'* op. cit. p. 78.

26 *High Level Conference on the Future of the European Court of Human Rights Brighton Declaration*, at para. 12(b), http://www.coe.int/en/20120419-brighton-declaration Accessed 22 April 2012.

27 *Lautsi & Ors v Italy* 30814/06 [2011] ECHR (GC).

28 *Scoppola v Italy* (No. 3) 126/05 [2012] ECHR (GC) 868: see especially paras 93–96.

29 David Davis and Jack Straw 'We must defy Strasbourg on prisoner votes' *The Sunday Telegraph*, 27 May 2012.

30 *Daily Mail*, 23 May 2012.

Christians, conscience and the law

introduction

Royal Navy Leading Medical Assistant Michael Lyons was told in May 2010 that he would be deployed to Afghanistan. However, he decided that it would be morally wrong to be part of British involvement there and applied for conscientious discharge. His application was refused and he began a written appeal to the Advisory Committee on Conscientious Objection. In September 2010, he attended obligatory operational deployment weapons training and refused to take part. After attempts to persuade him to change his mind, he was charged with intentionally disobeying a lawful command and sentenced at court martial to seven months' military detention, reduction to the rank of Able Seaman and dismissal.

He then appealed against the conviction and sentence on the grounds that the order was unlawful because it contravened his rights under Article 9 of the European Convention on Human Rights. Article 9(1) provides that:

> Everyone has the right to freedom of thought, conscience and religion; this right includes freedom to change his religion or belief and freedom, either alone or in community with others and in public or private, to manifest his religion or belief, in worship, teaching, practice and observance.

We shall examine the effect of Article 9 later in this essay but what is noteworthy is that it specifically provides that freedom of conscience is a human right. Did it help Michael Lyons in this case?

The answer was no. The Court of Appeal in England observed that in the case of *Bayatyan v Armenia*[1] the European Court of Human Rights had stated that conscientious objection motivated by a serious and insurmountable conflict between the obligation of military service and the individual's conscience or deeply-held religious or other beliefs could indeed engage Article 9. However, this simply meant that Article 9 was relevant. What was also significant were the words of Article 9(2), which qualify Article 9(1):

Freedom to manifest one's religion or beliefs shall be subject only to such limitations as are prescribed by law and are necessary in a democratic society in the interests of public safety, for the protection of public order, health or morals, or for the protection of the rights and freedoms of others.

Thus there is no absolute right under the European Convention of Human Rights to claim a right of conscientious objection to a law and in this case the Court of Appeal held that that the procedure for dealing with claims of conscientious objection satisfied the requirements in Article 9(2) above of being "prescribed by law" and "necessary in a democratic society". Further, it felt that if a person who had voluntarily joined the military sought to be discharged on the ground of conscientious objection then it was right that there should be a proper process for deciding whether or not that claim was well-founded. Until that had been established, Michael Lyons and others should continue to be subject to the requirements of military service and discipline; otherwise a claim would simply be an escape-route, regardless of the consequent risk to others, or whether or not the claim was well-founded.

I suggest that this case illustrates these important truths about conscience and the law:

(a) That the law does sometimes recognise a right of conscientious objection.

(b) That in a claim to such a right the law must be satisfied that it is indeed based on deeply held conscientious beliefs.

(c) That it follows that this right must be limited as otherwise everyone would just decide what laws they did not wish to apply to them and there would be anarchy. As the Judge Advocate, Alistair McGrigor, said in Michael Lyons' case: "Service personnel cannot pick and choose what service orders they carry out. Disobedience undermines the chain of command and service effectiveness."[2] The same, I suggest, applies to us all.

In this paper we will examine the two fundamental issues about claims based on conscience:

(a) What exactly is a conscientious belief?

(b) If a person holds such a belief, then when and in what circumstances can this justify a claim that the law does not and indeed should not apply to them?

what is a conscientious belief?

Let us start with the word 'conscience'. It is derived from the Latin 'conscientia' and means 'knowledge in oneself'. The word 'conscience' is often misunderstood. As Herbert McCabe puts it, "Nowadays we speak of someone 'consulting her conscience' rather as someone might consult a cookery book or a railway timetable."[3] Conscience is, he says, seen "as a private repository of answers to questions", which amount to a "personal set of guidelines" and nothing deeper.

It is this that Pope Benedict XVI refers to when he speaks of the identification of conscience "with the superficial consciousness and the reduction of man to his subjectivity", which leads to us being "completely dependent on the prevailing opinions of the day".[4] In simple terms a claim to a conscientious belief cannot and should not be just an assertion of my individual beliefs but must be based on something deeper and it is only when it is based on this 'something deeper' that it can truly be called a conscientious belief. The question, then, is where is this 'something deeper' to be found?

There are many biblical references to claims not to be bound by an unjust law as, in conscience, it is not binding. In the Second Book of Maccabees, Eleazar, the High Priest, was at a banquet and was forced to open his mouth to swallow pig's flesh. He refused and resolved instead to die "with honour rather than to live disgraced".[5] However, those in charge of the banquet took him aside and attempted to persuade him to adopt the stratagem of *appearing* to eat the meat as prescribed by the king but *in reality* to eat meat of a kind that he could eat. He roundly refused and declared that he would not bring "defilement and disgrace on my old age". Instead, he would die because "Even though I may avoid execution by man, I can never, living or dead, elude the grasp of the Almighty." With these words, we are told, he "went straight to the block". In modern times the Second Vatican Council emphasised in *Dignitatis Humanae* that the individual must not be forced to act against conscience nor be prevented from acting according to conscience, especially in religious matters, and based this right on the dignity of the human person.[6]

Note the words of Eleazar: "elude the grasp of the Almighty". Here Eleazar is making a link between a secular law and the higher law of God. An easy answer would be to say that for Christians this higher law is to be found in the precepts of Christianity and that a Christian would be justified in disobeying any law which conflicted with those precepts. This, however, takes us too far and too quickly, for it begs the question of what those precepts are, especially in the context of conscientious objection to a law.

For many Christians, and particularly Roman Catholics, these precepts are to be found in what is called the 'natural law'. Former Bishop of Oxford Richard Harries has described natural law as, "the concept of a natural order, or intrinsic moral order that can be grasped by rational minds."[7] The Second Vatican Council in *Gaudium et Spes* put it this way: "Deep within their consciences men and women discover a law which they have laid upon themselves and which they must obey".[8]

It is not only Christians who have this fundamental insight into what is good. In St. Paul's words:

> For instance, pagans who never heard of the Law but are led by reason to do what the law commands, may not actually 'possess' the Law but can be said to 'be' the law. They can point to the substance of the Law engraved on their hearts – they can call a witness, that is, their own conscience – they have accusation and defence, that is, their own mental dialogue.[9]

It is in this sense that Thomas Aquinas views what he calls *synderesis* as being what Pope Benedict XVI refers to as a kind of "primal remembrance of what is good and true".[10] Conscience is then regarded by Aquinas in the sense of being able to formulate a judgment in the light of this basic understanding of the good.[11]

We can draw three important conclusions from this:

(a) That, whatever term is used, there are fundamental moral precepts enshrined in Christianity and on the basis that a law offends these precepts we are entitled to refuse obedience to it on grounds of conscience.

(b) These fundamental moral precepts are, as St. Paul points out when he refers to 'pagans who never heard of the law', accessible to everyone, not just to Christians.

(c) It follows that Christians should support all justified claims based on conscientious objection to a law and not just those based overtly on Christian belief.

So, in Sophocles' *Antigone*, Antigone defies the order of Creon to leave her brother Polynices unburied and says in answer to Creon:

> That order did not come from God. Justice,
> That dwells with the Gods below, knows no such law,
> I did not think your edicts strong enough
> To overrule the unwritten unalterable laws
> Of God and heaven, you being only a man.
> They are not of today, but everlasting,
> Though where they came from, none of us can tell.[12]

Thus nearly 500 years before Christ we have the perfect statement of how there are fundamental moral precepts which transcend law and which justify disobedience to law on grounds of conscience. Christians would only change the last line: we do know where these "unwritten unalterable laws" come from.

when can claims based on a conscientious belief justify disobedience to a law?

The British Humanist Association (BHA) has said that the concept of conscientious objection acquires its problematic character from the conflict between two powerful, but diametrically opposing, moral requirements. One is the requirement to obey the law; the other, the requirement to follow the dictates of one's own conscience.[13]

Whilst Christians will not be likely to agree with the conclusions of the BHA, this is a clear way of putting it. When, then, can the moral requirement to follow one's conscience be justified?

In one sense, the answer to this question has already been given: disobedience to a law is justified when it conflicts with fundamental Christian principles. However, we need to go further and try to identify situations where this will be so. There is a consistent thread running through the writings of both St. Peter and St. Paul that wherever possible obedience should be given to the government. St. Paul writes, "you must obey all the governing authorities. Since all government comes from God, the civil authorities were appointed by God and anyone who resists authority is rebelling against God's decision, and such an act is bound to be punished."[14] That said, although St. Paul does advocate obedience to the authorities, he points out very clearly that "all government comes from God". This is where the Christian's right to refuse obedience to a law comes in.

A Christian can, I suggest, make such a claim in two types of case. The first will be where a Christian feels that the whole system of laws on which the State is based is so fundamentally anti-Christian that s/he cannot give any allegiance to its legal system at all. One of very many examples of heroic Christian witness in Nazi Germany is that of Frank Rienisch, a priest who was beheaded for refusing to take the military oath of allegiance on the grounds that, as he put it, "the present government is not an authority willed by God, but a nihilistic government that has attained its power only through force, lies and deceit."[15] The second will be where the Christian gives general assent to the laws of a State but refuses to do so in particular circumstances. One could say that if a government respects the principles of democracy and those of human rights then such claims will be rare.[16]

I suggest that Christian teaching requires that our legal system is underpinned by two fundamental principles and that these provide a touchstone against which a law can be judged. These are that it is the function of all governments to promote the common good and that the dignity of each person, as one made in the image of God, must be respected and never taken away.

these principles in practice

The difficulty with the two principles is, of course, that they are very broad. For example, I may feel that the law should allow those who are homeless and who squat in unoccupied buildings to claim ownership of them.[17] Thus I feel entitled on grounds of conscience to disobey the present law. The problem here is that others will identify other laws which they feel entitled to deny and there will be anarchy. The answer in most cases is not for Christians to claim to be able to defy the law but instead, by reasoned argument, to seek to amend it.

Yet this is not the complete answer. There will remain some laws that Christians will claim, on grounds of conscience, cannot and must not be obeyed. How do we identify them? For Roman Catholics the teachings of the Church expressed in its *magisterium* will be a sure guide, but other Christians will seek different ways to identify such laws. One is the principle of the German jurist Gustav Radbach (1870-1949) that where law stands in unbearable contradiction to the demands of justice the law must be set aside so that justice can be fulfilled. We could, I suggest, replace the phrase 'demands of justice' with 'fundamental Christian precepts'. How could we tell if a law stood in 'unbearable contradiction' to Christian principles? To some degree, this would be an instinctive reaction: one would, as a Christian, simply recoil from such a law and say: this just cannot stand!

how does UK law deal with claims based on conscientious objection?

English law has granted a right of conscientious objection for many years, but in very narrowly defined cases. Quakers were exempted from military service in 1803 and a general right of conscientious objection was introduced by the Military Service Act 1916. Sikhs are exempt from the requirement under the Road Traffic Act 1988 that motorcyclists must wear a helmet. One of the best known instances is probably S.4(1) of the Abortion Act 1967 which protects the right of conscientious objectors not to participate in an abortion which is lawful under this Act. The term 'participate' has been narrowly defined and in *Janaway v Salford Health Authority* it was held not to include a medical receptionist at Irlam Health

Centre who refused to type letters of referral from general practitioners to specialists with a view to termination of a woman's pregnancy.[18]

On this basis the General Medical Council has issued Guidance stating that the conscience clause does not apply to situations where a patient who is awaiting or has undergone a termination of pregnancy needs medical care, as this will not be *participation* in an abortion. There is also a duty to tell patients of their right to see another doctor. Moreover, the General Medical Council has now (2012) drafted new guidelines which state that doctors could be struck off for refusing to prescribe contraceptive pills to unmarried women. The guidelines state that it would be "discriminatory" for a doctor to refuse to prescribe the pill or the morning-after pill on the grounds that they do not believe in sex before marriage. Here is a clear case where there is a threat to conscientious beliefs and doctors are surely entitled to resist. A doctor who refuses to prescribe the morning after pill can say that what is at stake is the dignity of a human being whose life would be terminated by this. What about discrimination against the unborn child?

In a similar vein, the General Pharmaceutical Council has issued Guidance to pharmacists stating that if their beliefs prevent them from providing a pharmacy service, such as the morning after pill, then if they refer the patient to another pharmacy they must check that there is another pharmacist who can provide the pill and has the relevant stock.[19] The pharmacist might as well provide the pill anyway!

a way forward?

Where does this leave us today? I suggest four guidelines in this area:

(a) That wherever possible Christians give obedience to the law and work within it to secure the promotion of the common good and the dignity of each individual.

(b) That as a last resort Christians should claim a right not to be subject to a law which stands in "unbearable contradiction" to these principles.

(c) That in many cases it will be possible for reasonable adjustments to be made to a law to accommodate Christian beliefs and Christians should be alert to recognise these situations and to press for these reasonable adjustments.

(d) Christians should not just regard the question of conscience and the law in a negative light, in the sense of refusing to be bound by laws that go against conscience, but should promote a conscience-based approach to law itself.

We have already said something on the first two points, but what of the other two? These are large topics in themselves but we can sketch something on both of them.

There is already a precedent for the idea of making reasonable adjustments, as this was introduced by the Disability Discrimination Act 1995 and the law is now contained in the Equality Act 2010. S.20 requires reasonable adjustments to be made where "a provision, criterion or practice…puts a disabled person at a substantial disadvantage in relation to a relevant matter." Could a similar provision be introduced to cater for deeply held conscientious beliefs? Take, for example, the case of Lillian Ladele.[20] Ladele is a committed Christian who worked for Islington Council as a registrar of births, deaths and marriages. When the Civil Partnership Act came into force in December 2005 she was 'designated' a civil partnerships registrar. She objected and, as a result, was later subjected to a disciplinary investigation. In response, she lodged a claim for discrimination and harassment on grounds of religion and belief. Her claim failed.

The court said that the Equality Act (Sexual Orientation) Regulations 2007 obliges public authorities not to discriminate on the grounds of sexual orientation in the provision of goods and services and this extends to employees and office-holders, such as Lillian Ladele, who were to be considered 'public authorities' in their own right, regardless of any religious objections they might hold. However, Lillian Ladele had been a civil registrar before the Civil Partnership Act came into force and it would have been easy for Islington Council to exempt her from having to officiate at civil partnership ceremonies, as other councils did where they had employees who also refused to perform them, since other civil registrars could have performed the ceremonies. This would, I suggest, have been the perfect case for the application of a right for reasonable accommodations to be made to accommodate deeply held conscientious beliefs. In fact, at the time of writing (July 2012) Lillian Ladele is taking her case to the European Court of Human Rights on the ground that UK law has failed to protect her right to manifest her religion, contrary to Article 9 of the European Convention on Human Rights.[21] The problem with the use of the European Convention is that it depends on determined individuals bringing actions. How much better it would be if there was specific protection for their beliefs.

Finally, Christians can and should promote the idea of the law being based on conscience. In fact, a conscience-based jurisdiction already exists in English law and is known as 'equity'.[22] This system was originally applied by the medieval Chancellor and came to combine a concern for moderating the strict letter of the law with a focus on personal conscience.[23] An example of this can be seen in cases involving the family home where a house is bought in the name of one partner but the other has contributed to the purchase price. Although in strict law only the one in whose name the house is has any rights, equity may intervene and say that the house is held on trust for the partner who made a contribution to the price. In doing so, equity is in effect saying that it would be against conscience that a person with whose money a house was bought should have no rights over it. In fact, equity does not operate over the whole of English law, being mainly, but not exclusively, confined to property matters, but this idea of a conscience-based jurisdiction repays further study by Christians.

conclusion

When all is said and done, there will be cases where there is a stark choice to be made for the Christian: to abide by a law which offends fundamental Christian principles or not. In this case there is no room for fudge or compromise and the consequences of Christian witness must be squarely faced. Thomas More famously did this when faced with denying Henry VIII's Act of Supremacy. What rings down the centuries and is an inspiration to all Christians who follow him are his words following his conviction for denying the royal supremacy when he declared, "This indictment is grounded on an Act of Parliament directly contrary to the laws of God and his Holy Church", with the result that the indictment is "in law, amongst Christian men insufficient to charge any Christian man."[24]

It is the witness of those such as More and others that Christians and all who when faced with a direct conflict between the law and deeply held conscientious beliefs did not flinch but, in the last analysis, were prepared to die for these beliefs, that we must cherish and which can serve as an inspiration to us all.

references

1   *Bayatyan v Armenia* 23459/03 [2011] ECtHR (GC) (7 July 2011).

2   '"Conscientious objector" against Afghanistan war loses appeal', *The Guardian* (13 October 2011).

3   Herbert McCabe, *God Still Matters* (London and New York: Continuum, 2005) p. 152.

4   Pope Benedict XVI 'If you want peace…conscience and truth', in *Values in a Time of Upheaval* (San Francisco: Ignatius Press, 2006) p. 83.

5   II Maccabees 6.18-31. Quotations are from the New Jerusalem Version.

6   *Dignitatis Humanae* p. 2.

7   Richard Harries, *Faith in Politics* (London: Darton, Longman and Todd, 2010) p. 39. His whole discussion of this topic, at pp. 35-42, is well worth reading.

8   At para 16. I have used the version by Austin Flannery '*The Basic Sixteen Documents; Vatican Council II*' (Domnican Publications, 1995).

9   Romans 2.14-15.

10 Pope Benedict XVI 'If you want peace…' op. cit., p. 92.

11 My grateful thanks to Fr. Robert Ombres O.P., of Blackfriars, Oxford, for much illumination on Aquinas and conscience although he must not be thought responsible for what I have written.

12 I have used the translation in the edition in the Penguin Classics translated by E.F. Watling (Harmondsworth: Penguin, 1974).

13 Introduction to 'Right to Object? Conscientious Objection and Religious Conviction' BHA 2011.

14 Romans 13.1-3.

15 Frank Rienisch, *Dying We Live: Letters written by prisoners in Germany on the verge of execution* (London: Fontana Books, 1958) pp. 47-48. This marvellously inspiring little book contains many such accounts.

16 By human rights I am not advocating any particular system or classification of human rights but simply a respect for human rights as based on the Christian principle of the dignity of each person.

17 In fact such a claim can be made, based on Schedule 6 of the Land Registration Act 2002, but is very unlikely to succeed.

18 *Janaway v Salford Health Authority* (1988) AC 537.

19 *Catholic Herald* (12 August 2011).

20 *Ladele v London Borough of Islington* [2009] EWCA Civ 1357.

21 Another case is also being heard: that of Gary McFarlane who refused on religious grounds to provide psychosexual counselling to same sex couples.

22 Scottish lawyers would look at the notion of equity differently. See S. Allison 'Stair and Natural Law' *Law and Justice* 169 (2012) (forthcoming).

23   This notion comes from Aristotle. See Book 5, chapter 10 of the *Nicomachean Ethics* where the term *epieikeia* is used to describe it.

24   W. Roper *Life of Sir Thomas More* (London: London Folio Society, 1980) p. 89.

human rights – does faith matter?

Does faith matter to human rights? Is it right that you can't have human rights without faith of some sort or other? Of course it depends on what we mean by 'faith' and 'human rights'. Let's take the second of these terms first. The easy answer is, 'No, faith doesn't matter: the truth of human rights is evident in the legion of international human rights instruments that now embrace the whole world in their ethical web.' But of course this is entirely question-begging: where do these rights come from? What explains the existence of a right to this and not a right to that? Is anything that is in a human rights convention by definition a human right as a matter of truth as well as of law? Surely this cannot be the case.

It might be thought that the answer to these conundrums lies in stressing the underlying principle of respect for human dignity, in saying that human rights draw their strength and power from this fundamental idea that lies behind them – and there is as much plausibility as there is attractiveness to this. But if we are being honest with ourselves, human dignity is in itself something of a 'floating signifier', drawing its meaning from the culture that informs it rather than from a set of eternal verities that stand above the human fray, handing down instructions.

Suppose we actually succeed in tying down a 'true' meaning to 'respect for human dignity': what then? In a brilliant book a couple of years ago, *Justice for Hedgehogs*, the philosopher Ronald Dworkin sought to do exactly that.[1] Our dignity is rooted in showing ourselves self-respect, in taking our life seriously, in living up to our life. It is achieved through a life that aims for value, which has character and style, a "coherence endorsed by judgment" – in other words an authentic life.

Now Ronald Dworkin is not to be confused with Richard Dawkins. Though writing in the secular tradition, Dworkin is gentle on religion, admiring indeed. He does not oppose faith so long as it grows out of independent reflection. What Dworkin opposes is the kind of mechanical unthinking faith that merely obeys instruction from on high without ever asking why. But his focus on the individual and his insistence on the value of reason and reflection as the twin keys to the leading of a dignified life point to what may be a strong divergence between faith and secular traditions so far as human dignity and, therefore, human rights are concerned.

The difference between the two approaches can perhaps be best encapsulated by invoking an ancient distinction, that between subjective and objective right. Consider Dworkin's perspective once again. What matters is not where you end up but how you get there – it is more a procedural than a substantive moral theory. That is why Dworkin can respect even those whose engagement with religion – self-conscious and reasoned as he insists – has led them into practices, such as daily mass going, the Stations of the Cross, or the rosary, that he cannot understand, much less seek to emulate.

But must he also accept other kinds of conduct as evidencing a dignified life just because the person concerned has thought hard about it before doing it? What about the lazy couch-potato with three degrees who has decided, 'yes, this suits me just fine', or the person who has done the calculations and concluded that he'll get along best of all so long as he keeps his eye on his own material interests and thinks of no-one else. And if there is no deep sense of right conduct, how can we know what it is we ought to be reflecting on? For all our supposed commitment to reason, do we not just end up the slave to our passions, with reason a mere justifier of emotions rather than the driver of our life events?

In other words, the problem as I see it with even sophisticated secular reflections on dignity like those of Ronald Dworkin is this: how can a procedural approach to dignity of this sort avoid collapsing into a subjectivity which turns all liberty into licence so long as you have thought about it first?

This is certainly where faith matters. I am interested in the Catholic Church because it is the faith I know, but what follows may well apply to other organised religions as well. This Church has an approach to dignity which insists that it is about the flourishing of the person for sure, but that the success of any person can never just be in the eye of the beholder in this way. There is inevitably a moral dimension. Archbishop Vincent Nichols put this very well in a lecture at the London School of Economics, when he said that, "to be human is to be a meaning-seeking creature", and

> to be fully human is to be more than an individual – it is to be a person-in-relationship, self-transcendent, creative and emergent. These are the very bonds that enable us to understand and fulfil our freedom to be ourselves."[2]

What the Archbishop is engaging in here is more than just an argument, a point of view that tries to win in an open debate among equal perspectives. For, to Archbishop Nichols and his Church, "it is *homo religiosus*' who is truly happy, truly human because this person has recognised the deepest reality of their nature." Unlike the secular human rights advocate I have just been describing, there is here "a deepest reality" to reach down to. As the Archbishop puts it, "what religious freedom…reinforces is an understanding of 'human dignity' as a capacity to 'transcend one's own materiality and to seek truth.'"

There does appear to be a foundational difference here between faith and secular perspectives on human rights. The Catholic Church is confident that it is worth searching for the "definitive behind the provisional" and that finding such truth (or even simply looking for it) is the key to a successful and, therefore, a dignified life.[3] Protagonists of human rights outside any faith tradition are, by contrast, in something of a bind: their language proclaims a belief in truth the possibility of which their secular, postmodern selves feel duty bound simultaneously to deny.

human rights and the Church: a shared agenda

Why don't we just ignore the foundational divide between faith and secular perspectives on human rights? So what if these two versions of human rights and human dignity get to the same truths by radically different routes? Not everyone must take the same route to right behaviour. In an address in France in 2008, His Holiness Pope Benedict identified one of the roles of the Church as being the "creation of a basic ethical consensus in society" and he returned to this theme often during his visit to Britain in 2010, particularly in his address at Westminster Hall.[4]

It is undoubtedly the case that faith and human rights groups share much in common: they fight for justice in the same way, they care about the poor and the underdog, the maligned and the outsider, the oppressed everywhere, with similar levels of passion and compassion. Looking at their actions on the street you cannot tell which is a priest or nun and which a human rights worker. In the eyes of God no doubt they are – all of them – both. There is already a strong consensus on what a commitment to human rights entails, encapsulated in the international documents on human rights. The Church and civil society also share the same values which serve to underpin and energise the human rights campaigns to which they both feel able to contribute in equal intensity, albeit, as I have just acknowledged, driven by different kinds of motives for their shared humanitarianism.

I know that this emphasis on commonality may sound odd, misplaced even. There are those in the Church (and indeed in secular society) who see war where I see peace, whose first image is of a field of battle rather than of two forces working together towards the common good. Of course, there are differences of emphasis and I will come to those shortly. But first we should notice some basic facts. The human rights model that pertains across Europe is strongly supportive of Christian practice.[5] The European Convention on Human Rights guarantees a right to freedom of religious belief and (within sensible limits) to the manifestation of that belief. The EU has sophisticated systems for the prohibition of discrimination on religious grounds. Closer to home, the Human Rights Act not only embeds the European Convention in UK law but goes out of its way to say (in section 13) that

> if a court's determination of any question arising under this Act might affect the exercise by a religious organisation (itself or its members collectively) of the Convention right to freedom of thought, conscience and religion, it must have particular regard to the importance of that right.

Nor is the European Court of Human Rights the secularist bogey-man of the anxious believer's imagination. What is interesting about the Court's ruling on abortion law in Ireland is that it is much more about Ireland's hypocrisy in promising to enact an abortion law and failing to do so than it is about a women's right to privacy trumping that of the unborn.[6] And so far as the furore over the presence of crucifixes in state-school classrooms in Italy is concerned, the judgment of the Chamber of the Court on 3 November 2009 ruling this a breach of human rights received (rightly) a great deal of attention, the Grand Chamber's decision overturning that ruling (handed down on 15 March 2011 by a majority of 15 votes to 2) rather less so. As a result of this definitive ruling, we now know that such matters as these are for the states themselves to decide, so long as the emblems of faith are not being used to engage in the indoctrination of pupils.[7] But the media have let the resolution of this supposed crisis in secular-faith relations drift quietly by.

There is an important point here which these cases support, concerning the importance of religion in the public sphere. It is something that the Catholic Church must continue to stress, not only on its own account but also on behalf of less embedded religions, ones that are more vulnerable to being condemned for not being British enough for the government's taste, for mixing too much with their own kind and for not behaving as the authorities believe good Britons should. There is a memory in the Catholic Church in Britain of what it is like to be an outsider, to be associated with terrorism and identified with hostile forces within the state. Catholics in Britain should draw on that memory now to offer a veil of solidarity to fellow followers of a path marked out by faith.

It is right that human rights and the church should join in promoting a culture that is more than merely 'tolerant' of religion but which positively celebrates faith as an important enrichment in many people's lives. I believe that an authentic secular approach to human rights does exactly this. And the days are long gone when one church sought to triumph at the expense of another: in these days of materialist hegemony, more unites than divides our major faith communities.

It is also at least 400 years too late for any European Church to assert its control over peoples who have developed new allegiances – to the democratic state, to universal human rights, to law – which can exist in parallel with religious authority but which are definitely and rightly not subject to it. If Christians – and perhaps even some Christian leaders – sometimes give the impression that they regret this, that the world of the Papal Monarchy or of Calvin's Zurich would be more agreeable to them, then I have to say that I profoundly disagree with them. I am a Catholic who gives thanks to those men and women of the past whose struggles helped achieve the secular culture within which my faith is practised today.

human rights and the Church: points of tension

Many of the tensions that do remain between faith-based and secular approaches to human rights derive from the way in which the understanding of what makes a whole person and a successful life has deepened in this secular world in a way that has not (perhaps not yet?) been acknowledged in much of the religious sphere. But even here those whose human rights commitments are informed by faith do not always share the point of view of their religious masters. I am thinking now in particular of the advances in our understanding of gender and sexual orientation that have been among the great civilising triumphs of my lifetime.

When I was born women knew their place and queers stayed firmly in the closet. Now women are used to being given the opportunities historically open only to men. We have had a woman prime minister and there is a woman on the United Kingdom's newly established Supreme Court. It is now also widely accepted across civil society that sexual orientation is part of what we are and that our success as a person, our flourishing in our space in the world, is greatly enhanced by our being able to express ourselves sexually as much as in other ways that flow out of our essence.

It strikes me that some of this at least has seemed to pass religion by. Certainly the Catholic Church has not got close to taking these changes to her heart. Women are still prevented from answering their vocations in a way that would allow them to become priests rather than nuns. We insist on this, whatever the price that is paid by the individual in terms of a stunting of their capacity to succeed in their life, to thrive as their conscience and their prayers demand: whatever the price of this denial we seem willing to pay it. But why? Are the feminist insights and the advances that these made possible in the second half of the twentieth century a passing fad?

It is not just women priests of course, but married priests as well. The secular human rights campaigner has always been puzzled by this but he or she is now completely dumbfounded: you can be a married priest as long as you have been an Anglican first. Human rights law has always taken the view that certain rights can be breached in a discriminatory way so long as the discriminatory judgment can be justified on rational grounds. But such discrimination is exposed where the basis for it is not grounded in a reason recognisable to civil society. When we recall that the Human Rights Act includes a right to marry (in article 12) with a prohibition against discrimination (in article 14), it reminds us that it is lucky for the Church that civil society has chosen to immunise it from the effects of human rights law (another example of favourable treatment by the way) because the current position would surely not pass muster.

There is one other field of engagement in which church teaching and the contemporary secular human rights movement part ways, and that is on human sexuality and, in particular, homosexuality. Of course there is a strong positive attitude being taken in Westminster diocese and I applaud that and the support shown by Archbishop Vincent and his clergy to gay Catholics in this community of believers. But London is (I am tempted to say 'sadly') not the whole Church.

In a statement made in the course of the proceedings of the Human Rights Council held in Geneva in March 2011, Archbishop Silvano Tomasi (the Permanent Representative of the Holy See to the UN in Geneva) spoke about "some unnecessary confusion about the meaning of the term 'sexual orientation'".[8] He went on to say that the "ordinary meaning" of the term "refers to feelings and thoughts, not to behaviour", and that "for the purposes of human rights law, there is a critical difference between feelings and thoughts, on the one hand, and behaviour on the other." While feelings and thoughts should never be punished, says Archbishop Tomasi, "states can, and must regulate behaviours, including various sexual behaviours." This is because human sexuality, "like any voluntary activity, possesses a moral dimension" and denying this (as with those who cannot see sexuality as composed solely of a "complete and lifelong mutual devotion of a man and a woman in marriage") "undermines ultimately his/her ontological dignity." On this account 'dignity' has become something outside the individual, a condition to strive towards, however difficult (or even impossible) personal circumstances make this.

I am bound to say that the secular human rights advocate simply does not understand dignity in this way. Recalling the subjective dimension to dignity, and refusing to accept that the expression of a homosexual orientation is merely the indulgence of an immoral licentiousness, the secular protagonist of human rights sees the expression of one's sexuality as a vital way of being oneself, of living an authentic and flourishing life. It is part of the core, a central piece of the jigsaw that makes up the self. Of course, the law can and does regulate paedophilia and incest (the two examples of legal regulation compatible with human rights law to which Archbishop Tomasi refers, as though there were ever any serious question of either being decriminalised) but what human rights law insists is not to be prohibited is the expression of sexual feelings between consenting adults either of the same or (outside of marriage) of different genders.

The Roman Catholic Church rightly seeks to influence civil society. Its commitment to true multiculturalism, to supporting all branches of society in their living of collectively authentic lives while not impacting negatively the rights of others, is both laudable and important. I agree, too, that the secular perspective has much to gain from reflecting more deeply on what it means by freedom, and on how life can be made meaningful in a world consumed by materialism – financial, sexual and relational. The shallowness of all of this is evident even to those for whom it currently forms the whole pool of their endeavour. You do not have to be a believer in a mainstream faith to know that there is more to life than what so often seems to be all that is available. The Churches and the Catholic Church in particular have so much to offer.

But getting to an ethical consensus is a two-way process. The Church must listen as well as speak. Its current position on women and on sexuality is so dogmatic, so removed from the life experience of so many *bona fide* seekers after dignity, that it risks drowning out the vital news that the Church can bring on how a good life is possible and how there can be more to living than the latest pair of shoes or celebrity pseudo-crisis. The real enemy is emptiness, not the wrong kind of love.

This essay is based on a talk given on 30 March 2011 in Westminster Cathedral Hall as part of the Faith Matters series.

references

1   Ronald Dworkin, *Justice for Hedgehogs* (Cambridge, MA: Harvard University Press, 2011).

2   'Good Life in Hard Times', 2 March 2011: http://www2.lse.ac.uk/publicEvents/events/2011/20110302t1830vSZT.aspx.

3   Address of His Holiness Benedict XVI on his meeting with representatives of the world of culture, Paris 12 September 2008.

4   See Address at Elysée Palace, Paris (12 September 2008) http://www.vatican.va/holy_father/benedict_xvi/speeches/2008/september/documents/hf_ben-xvi_spe_20080912_parigi-elysee_en.html; and Address at Westminster Hall, City of Westminster, (17 September 2010) http://www.vatican.va/holy_father/benedict_xvi/speeches/2010/september/documents/hf_ben-xvi_spe_20100917_societa-civile_en.html.

5   See Ronan McCrea, *Religion and the Public Order of the European Union* (Oxford: Oxford University Press, 2010).

6   A, B and C v Ireland [2010] ECHR 2032.

7   *Lautsi v Italy* (Application no. 30814/06), 18 March 2011.

8   http://www.zenit.org/article-32108?l=english.

human rights, conscience and the public good

human rights theory and Christian thinking

Much modern thinking in relation to issues of equality and discrimination is based upon human rights. Human rights theory is helpful in asserting that there are universal values derived from the nature of human beings, but there are significant difficulties with a secular view of human rights. There is no common agreement as to the source of the rights and, if we cannot agree how rights arise or how they are conferred, it is difficult to agree what they should be. There is also no common basis for a discussion about the way in which rights should be applied, in particular in relation to the precedence to be accorded to conflicting rights.

In Christian thinking, rights exist either as the expression of a gift from God upon which human beings must not trespass, for instance the right to (or sanctity of) life, or as the result of the obligations which human beings owe to each other, which in turn flow from the duties they owe to their creator. They reflect the two-fold duties of a human being to love God and to love neighbour.

The assertion of rights in themselves, without recognising and basing the rights upon the duties from which they flow, can lead to injustice. Human rights theory fails to draw out adequately the distinction which Cicero makes (quoting Zeno) between things that are materially advantageous and things that contribute to the common good.[1] Rights, by their nature, whether they are defensive (to stop others doing something), or are in the nature of a claim to an interest or a good, are a reflection of human autonomy in that their basis is centred upon individuals and their personal treatment. This means that, both in principle and in practice, the rights need to be asserted and enforced by those who have been prejudiced by an infringement of the rights. This can automatically disenfranchise those who, because they are weak or vulnerable, are unable to do so. And, in a number of cases, a concept of rights cannot be appropriate because it is impossible, in theory as well as in practice, for the person affected to exercise a right. Those who are mentally incapacitated, comatose or dead cannot assert their rights, though others may nevertheless have duties towards them. It is only possible to explain why it is right to carry out the wishes of a dead person in terms of a duty, not in terms of rights.

In practical terms, even on the assumption that it is appropriate to define particular aspirations for human beings in terms of rights, some so-called rights may at particular points in time be simply undeliverable. For example, it does not make sense to claim that there is an absolute legal right to food and water in circumstances where, immediately following a natural disaster, no-one is physically capable of delivering them. There would, however, be a moral duty on others to do all they can to deliver humanitarian aid and that aid may extend beyond the provision of food and water.

Further, because they are personal to individuals, rights can be released by consent, but such consent may be wrongly given. An elderly person may freely consent to relinquishing the right to life because they do not want to be a burden on their relations (while not being coerced in any way). But they may make the wrong choice in purely human terms (quite apart from any Christian belief in the sanctity of life), both for themselves and for their close family.

The Christian perception that duties precede rights connects with the belief in a creator. Duties do not exist unless they are owed to a person. For the Christian, duties are owed to the creator as well as to other human beings. This is important because, as mentioned above, people can be persuaded to absolve others of their duties towards them, or to give up the rights that stem from such duties. For instance, there is a duty to God, as well as to other people, to live and to sustain life, and the reflection of this duty is the right to life. So, in Christian thinking, a duty to sustain life cannot be released by a person contemplating suicide or by others who might be affected by the suicide, even if they could all be identified and were able to give their consent.

Thus, whereas Christian thinking would hold that there is a duty not to kill an unborn human being (whether or not that human being has any rights or the means to exercise them), human rights legislation does not recognise that a human being has any human rights until birth. The necessity of asserting a right in law, rather than requiring compliance with a duty, means that the beneficiary of the right needs to have the status in law of a person, and so the current law does not recognise an unborn child as having the human rights of a born child.

In relation to non-discrimination, the arguments expressed in terms of secular human rights can, by focussing on the effect on those affected by the alleged discrimination, bypass issues of the public good. One of the reasons for this is that rights can be seen as absolute and, once invoked, can automatically trump other concerns. Further, the issue of the public good may not have had an adequate discussion when legislation was introduced. A minority group should only be accorded protection in law from discrimination by virtue of the characteristics or beliefs of that group where it has been decided, after examination of all the evidence, that those characteristics and beliefs are good, or at least neutral, and it is in the public interest to protect them. We can illustrate some of the practical difficulties which spill out from the secular theory of human rights in the context of non-discrimination by examining some recent developments of English law related to the manifestation of belief.

living out beliefs

Christian thinking is based upon the gift of free will by God who gives individuals the choice as to whether or not to believe and trust in him. This foundational principle supports the free expression of beliefs and opinions. Christian teaching is that government is also given for the purpose of protection. So, in some cases, where a manifestation of belief injures others, it may need to be curtailed. However, a person's ability to hold a belief, as opposed to acting upon it, should normally be unquestioned.

It can be said that nearly all belief requires some manifestation, if only that of gathering with others to share the belief. In practice, however, the requirements of the Christian faith go beyond this. As James, the brother of Jesus, put it, "faith without works is dead".[2] According to the European Convention on Human Rights, freedom of thought, conscience and religion is a right that can be limited by governments "in the interests of public safety, for the protection of public order, health or morals, or for the protection of the rights and freedoms of others".[3]

employees of the State and public functions

In the UK those holding certain public offices have not been allowed to hold beliefs and act upon them when these beliefs are contrary to government policy on civil partnerships. An example is the case of registrar Lillian Ladele.[4] The issue in the legal case centred around whether Ms. Ladele, a registrar, had a right to decline to perform a civil partnership ceremony on the basis of a religious belief. It was decided that she could not do so and, therefore, was not unfairly dismissed for being unwilling to perform the ceremony. Part of the reasoning of the Court of Appeal in this case was that to decline to act was discrimination against the persons who required the ceremony. Although this conclusion had a basis in the relevant Regulations, the logic can be questioned, since it was the public authority which was providing the service and not Ms Ladele herself in a personal capacity. Thus only the public authority (and not Ms Ladele) could fail to provide the services. If the public authority was able to find a replacement for Ms. Ladele, then there would be no discrimination, particularly since those affected need not be aware of her disinclination. So, although the court applied the relevant law in terms of discrimination, the substantive question should have been whether a public servant should be allowed to hold the belief that homosexual unions are wrong and decline to perform the ceremony. Medical doctors are currently permitted in law to refuse to perform abortions, but this ability to exercise freedom of conscience does not extend to issues in relation to civil partnerships.

In Ladele, given the existing law in relation to discrimination, the Court of Appeal may not have been in a position to consider the wider questions of the public good or the role of the State. Had it done so, it might have been in a better position to conclude that Ms Ladele's beliefs should have been accommodated. Ms Ladele's beliefs were not irrational and represented those of a traditional faith system which, in this case, was reflected in the law until the introduction of civil partnerships. Further, the Council could have found others to perform the functions so that gay couples would not have been prejudiced. In the event, the argument in relation to freedom of conscience was raised but rejected. Justice Laws said that in a multi-faith society no religious belief was worthy of any particular protection since to provide it would be "deeply unprincipled". So it was not possible to examine whether there was a wider public good in Christian values.

Another example of the power of the State in relation to belief is the case of the Johns, a husband and wife who are experienced foster carers.[5] The local Council delayed in approving them as respite carers of children while questioning them about their Christian beliefs about homosexuality. The effect of the court judgment in this case was that the local authority had the right to determine its own diversity policy with the effect that certain people may be disqualified from being foster carers by virtue of a belief that homosexuality is wrong.

It is, of course, right that the State should have regard to the interests of the child and seek to put a foster child in a suitable family. In doing this it is not wrong for the State to consider the beliefs of the foster parents as one of the matters to be taken into account. If, for instance, the Johns had been neo-Nazis or violent extremists, the local authority would have been right to decline to place a child with them. In this case, despite some prompting from Counsel for the Johns, there was no examination in the judgment as to whether the Christian beliefs of the Johns were in fact (taking into account the whole of their beliefs) good for the children, who should have been the primary concern. Indeed, the judge said that, "we sit as secular judges serving a multicultural community of many faiths". He went on to say that "the aphorism that Christianity is part of the common law of England is mere rhetoric." It was assumed that the Council's policies in relation to diversity must be agreed by the Johns. Nor was there any consideration of the extent to which it was reasonable for the State to require compliance with the policies, or of the wider effect of the requirements of the State which could result in the exclusion of many Christians from the provision of foster care. It should also be noted that, though they were remunerated by the local authority for their foster care, the Johns were private individuals offering foster care in their own home, and not public servants performing a public office. They were, therefore, in a different position to public servants who might be said to owe some duty to the State.

non-discrimination in employment

The Equality Act 2010 requires non-discrimination in appointments on the grounds of religious belief and sexual orientation. There is a limited exemption in the case of religious belief where the employer has "an ethos based on religion or belief" and there is also an occupational requirement for the employee to have a belief based upon that ethos. The exemption may be construed quite narrowly and may be confined to those employees performing teaching functions or rituals. The exemption does not take into account the fact that those working for a Christian organisation in a non-teaching capacity, for instance administration, may be motivated by their Christian belief to uphold certain standards. Both the employees and the organisation for which they work would want this motivation to be reflected in the beliefs and behaviour of all employees and in the practices of the organisation.

There is also a limited exclusion in relation to discrimination on the grounds of sexual orientation which applies to employment for the purposes of "organised religion" where the requirement is necessary to comply with "the strongly held religious convictions of a significant number of the religion's followers". The scope of organised religion is narrow since this is not the same as a religious organisation and therefore only applies to established religious denominations and not, for instance, to a Christian charity.

In this legislation, the perspective of the public good has been lacking. The requirements of the Act conflict with the principle of freedom of association, which is generally recognised as a public good. This is the ability of private citizens to associate with whom they please and is relevant here since the bodies affected are private, not public, organisations.

An anomalous aspect of these laws is that discrimination is permitted in the case of beliefs that do not qualify as religious, such as political or other ideological beliefs or opinions about other subjects. So, understandably, a political organisation, in selecting whom to employ, is allowed to discriminate against a person who does not hold the beliefs of that organisation. However, a religious organisation is limited in its ability to do the same thing.

A legal requirement of non-discrimination in employment on the grounds of gender, race or colour is generally accepted on the grounds that it promotes racial cohesion, but belief and sexual practice are different from these characteristics. Religion and sexual practice are not permanent defining characteristics similar in nature to that of ethnic origin. Ethnicity cannot be changed, but beliefs may be debated and practice altered.

the provision of services

Similar non-discrimination requirements apply to the provision of services.

Thus it has been held that a Christian bed and breakfast proprietor cannot reserve double beds exclusively for married couples. He is not permitted to do so, on the grounds that he is discriminating against homosexual couples, even if he would behave in the same way towards unmarried heterosexual couples. In this case, it makes no difference to the legal analysis that the homosexual couple alleging discrimination could easily have obtained the relevant facilities elsewhere, so that in practice the exercise of their right (if such it is) to manifest their orientation was unhindered.

The effect of the legislation is to render the manifestation of a certain belief unlawful, in this case the exercise of the Christian belief, without reference to the practical effect of the manifestation of the belief on those affected, which may have been immaterial. Nor can equality legislation that is framed in terms of discrimination and human rights balance the interests of those alleging discrimination against the benefits of freedom of belief in the context of the wider public good.

difficulties with reasonable accommodation for belief

There is a current proposal by a number of Christian organisations that there should be reasonable accommodation for issues of conscience. The intention might seem to balance fairly the conflicting rights of the different interest groups. The proposal would appear to be a pragmatic one in a society that appears to have rejected a number of Christian values. It needs to be understood, however, that giving Christians or other faith groups reasonable accommodation in the expression of their beliefs does not address the more fundamental question, which is whether the relevant belief is consistent with a rational view of the public good. There is a concern that it may be difficult for the Courts, which have now taken the view that no belief system has any particular status or value compared with another, to resist calls for a multiplicity of beliefs to be accommodated. For example, a Muslim believer employed in a supermarket might object to handling pork on the grounds that it is a matter of religious belief, and that others could be employed to perform these tasks. It could then be argued that this is comparable with a doctor declining to perform an abortion and that his belief should be accommodated. Thus, while the concept of reasonable accommodation may be a helpful means to achieve compromises in practice, it is still necessary for there to be some criteria to determine what beliefs are acceptable and should therefore be accommodated and, where there are conflicts, how these should be resolved.

conclusion

Issues of discrimination and human rights throw up fundamental questions relating to the public good and the role of government in allowing the manifestation of belief systems and the exercise of conscience. The current law does not allow consideration of the public good, but this could provide the context for a fair balance to be struck between competing interests which are often framed in terms of human rights. Christian belief in the duties to a creator and love of neighbour in community can provide a basis for examining what is the common good. A secular view of human rights focuses upon the interests of individuals and also provides a rationale for governments to require its beliefs (framed, for instance, in terms of diversity) to be accepted by its citizens. A Christian concept of the common good is a more compelling framework for addressing issues of conscience and can address some of the structural weaknesses in the theory and application of secular human rights.

references

1 Cicero, *The Laws*, Book One (Oxford: Oxford World Classics, 2008) p. 117.

2 James 2.20, Authorised Version.

3 See Article 9(2) on the website of the European Court of Human Rights: http://www.echr.coe. int/NR/rdonlyres/D5CC24A7-DC13-4318-B457-5C9014916D7A/0/ENG_CONV.pdf.

4 Ladele v Islington LBC, [2009] EWCA Civ 1357.

5 *R. (on the application of Johns) v Derby City Council* [2011] EWHC 375 (Admin). The legal processes surrounding the case were somewhat complex, since the parties sought a declaration in the form of answers to defined questions, though the matter was framed as a judicial review of a decision that had not yet taken place.

the connection between law and justice in the natural law tradition

Law, we are told, is a system of rules, created by men to govern human behaviour. Students of law are introduced to legal systems and become familiar with varied sources of law – legislative, judicial and executive in character. There are undoubtedly prescriptive human rules that govern people, set up by public authorities, which are advertised as being for the common good. These appear as visible, socially-constructed systems in different jurisdictions and even as international systems across jurisdictions. But is this all there is to law? Is law merely a human construct subject to flux, different according to time and place? Or must law, in its fullest sense, be seen as an activity that needs to be interpreted aright, binds the human conscience and is answerable to certain universal and timeless demands? Is there any natural moral law common to all, universal and timeless?

the classical natural law tradition

Sophocles spoke of "the immutable unwritten laws of Heaven [which] were not born today nor yesterday; they die not; and none knoweth whence they sprang."[1] Cicero wrote that justice is "that Supreme Law which had its origin ages before any written law existed or any State had been established."[2] He rejected any cultural relativism or any form of legal positivism, affirming the folly of such an outlook, and regarded "most foolish of all…the belief that everything decreed by the institutions of laws of a particular country is just." According to him, justice binds together human society and is established by right reason:

> There is one single justice. It binds together human society and has been established by one, single law. That law is right reason in commanding and forbidding. One who does not acknowledge this law is unjust, whether it has been written down anywhere or not.[3]

For Cicero there was an eternal source of law which exists apart from what is written down or socially constructed by men. This true and primal law, right reason, exists in eternity and simultaneously with the divine mind. Accordingly, law is not entirely humanly constructed. There is an intrinsic connection between law and justice, and justice is bound up with an eternal source that is right reason.

This reason did not first become Law when it was written down, but when it first came into existence; and it came into existence simultaneously with the divine mind. Wherefore the true and primal Law, applied to command and prohibition, is the right reason of supreme Jupiter.[4]

Cicero's recognition of "right reason in harmony with nature" led him to conclude that "all peoples at all times will be embraced by a single and eternal and unchangeable law; and there will be, as it were, one lord and master of us all – the God who is the author, proposer, and interpreter of that law." For Cicero, the refusal to recognize this "right reason" results in a rejection of one's nature as a human being, a thing that attracts serious consequences:

Whoever refuses to obey it will be turning his back on himself. Because he has denied his nature as a human being he will face the gravest penalties for this alone, even if he succeeds in avoiding all the other things that are regarded as punishments.[5]

The death of Socrates at the hands of unjust oligarchs who required that he collaborate with injustice reminds us that the Platonic understanding of law is embedded in a metaphysics that challenges any modern hedonism or social Darwinism. Since transient bodily suffering compares as nothing to moral evil which affects the soul, suffering is preferable to doing evil. The doctrine that "it is better to suffer wrong than to do it" is widely known as the Socratic principle:

Men of Athens, do not interrupt, but hear me;…if you kill such a one as I am, you will injure yourselves more than you will injure me. [My persecutors] will not injure me: they cannot; for it is not in the nature of things that a bad man should injure a better than himself. I do not deny that he may, perhaps, kill him, or drive him into exile, or deprive him of civil rights; and he may imagine, and others may imagine, that he is doing him a great injury: but in that I do not agree with him; for the evil… of unjustly taking away another man's life – is greater far.[6]

For Socrates, his persecutors were in far greater danger than he was, for what they imperilled was their very eternal souls, while he stood only to suffer transient pain:

The difficulty, my friends, is not in avoiding death, but in avoiding unrighteousness; …I depart hence condemned by you to suffer the penalty of death, and they, too, go their ways condemned by the truth to suffer the penalty of villainy and wrong.[7]

That there is a natural law – immutable, eternal, universal and unchangeable – governing man is an idea that arguably appears in numerous sacred traditions.

eternal law: source of natural physical laws and natural moral laws

In sacred scripture, the thought that there are laws governing the natural sciences, as well as moral laws, has been seen as implying a creator and regulator of all things, and an eternal source of these laws. Equally it raises the disputed question of the place of miracles, or the suspensions of those laws, in the natural scheme of things.

In the same way, sacred scripture speaks of Divine Wisdom as directing all actions and movements. The Psalms say, "He hath made a decree and it shall not pass away".[8] Creatures, both rational and non-rational alike, are subject to the power of divine reason. In the book of Proverbs it is said, "He compassed the sea with its bounds, and set a law to the waters, that they should not pass their limits."[9] Law, then, according to sacred scripture, may be thought to govern natural events as well as human societies. The laws of science, according to scripture, derive from that eternal source of all things. Laws govern nature, as understood scientifically. The law that governs both physical and moral laws, and is identified in revelation, is often spoken of as the eternal law.

St Thomas Aquinas speaks of an eternal law which governs both the physical and moral orders.[10] Divine law is that law which has its source in the Eternal Law. It is given by divine revelation in the Old and New Testaments. This law is intelligible to humans using reason, is described in the Bible, and embraces both physical nature and rational agents. To limit law to that binding rational agents alone is inappropriately to adumbrate law's binding force and wrongly adopt a humanistic and subjectivized vision of law. It is this broader understanding of law that allows us to observe the law that existed from eternity in the mind of God. When we understand God as the lawgiver and see the fullness of the universe, the earth, sun, stars and planets, of men and angels, of all things visible and invisible, a community under the authority of the lawgiver and source of all things who is God, we are better able to understand the power, dominion and authority of God. This fuller understanding of law allows us also to make sense of the divinity and incarnation of Christ as witnessed by the Holy Gospel according to St John, "In the beginning was the Word, and the Word was with God and the Word was God."[11]

The eternal law is distinct again from the natural law strictly understood. Reason in human beings is capable of apprehending certain general principles implanted in human nature. The first principle of the natural law is "good is to be done and pursued, and evil avoided".[12] All other precepts of natural law rest upon this. What Aquinas seems to mean is that the several precepts of natural law are specifications of this precept, which is highly abstract. To define human law, a Thomist must refer to natural law. Aquinas says that it is from the precepts of the natural law, as from general and indemonstrable principles, that the human reason needs to proceed to certain particular determinations of the laws. These particular determinations, devised by human reason, are called human laws.[13]

The natural law is law with moral content, more general than human law. Natural law deals with necessary rather than with changeable things. In explicating human laws, human practical reason moves from the general principles implanted in the natural order to the contingent commands of human law. Natural law is more perfect than human laws, because of the variable content of human laws.

Human laws are applications of natural law and cannot deviate entirely from the spirit of the natural law, as applied to the time and place of the human law's promulgation. If a human law does deviate in this way, if it is not a proper and rationally defensible application of the natural law, then it is a perversion of law, which is to say, it is a law in name only.[14] In the words of Augustine, "*Lex iniusta non est lex*": An unjust law is not a law.[15]

the medieval natural law tradition

The natural law tradition is also arguably to be found in Maimonides[16] and the writings of Avicenna[17] and Averroes[18]. Certainly Aquinas thought as much and appealed to reason in his discussions of the writings of these thinkers. Maimonides, for example, whom Aquinas deferentially refers to as Rabbi Moses, in his *Eight Chapters on Ethics*, suggests, like Plato and Aristotle, that like the body, the soul can be diseased or healthy and that those with diseased souls need to seek the wise rulers, who are physicians of the soul. Maimonides holds that Judaic law is based on a sound account of the soul and the conditions needed for its perfection. Chief among them is the attainment of a mean between extremes. Echoing Aristotle, he writes in *Eight Chapters*, "The virtues are states of the soul and settled dispositions in the mean between two bad states, one of which is excessive, the other deficient."[19] Later, in the first book of the *Mishneh Torah*, he follows up by saying, "The right way is the mean in every one of a person's character traits."[20] A similar sentiment is expressed earlier in the *Mishneh Torah*[21], when Maimonides discusses the need to study physics and metaphysics. He concludes with praise for those who are lowly of spirit:

> When a man reflects on these things, studies all these created beings, from the angels and spheres down to human beings and so on, and realizes the divine wisdom manifested in them all, his love for God will increase, his soul will thirst, his very flesh will yearn to love God. He will be filled with fear and trembling.[22]

The Islamic thinker, Ibn Rushd or Averroes, addressed by Aquinas as 'the Commentator' such was his respect for his work, in *On the Harmony of Religions and Philosophy*, supplies a poetic account of the argument from design.[23] To observe the points of union in the natural law tradition between the great sacred traditions is not to suggest that there are no differences between the religions. Manifestly there are. Teachings in relation to marriage, family, divorce, liturgical practice, and ritual can all depend on both the content and the perceived place of revelation. However, that there are points of unity is undeniable. For Averroes there is no contradiction between the aims of religion and philosophy. Renowned for his translations and commentaries on the works of Aristotle, he rejects Al Ghazali's conclusion that philosophy has the propensity to undermine religion and Islamic teaching in particular, as not merely mistaken but misplaced. Avicenna affirms in his thesis *On Love*, that:

> Every being which is determined by a design strives by nature toward its perfection, i.e. that goodness of reality which ultimately flows from the reality of the Pure Good, and by nature it shies away from its specific defect which is the evil in it, i.e. materiality and non-being, for every evil results from attachment to matter and non-being.[24]

Although Avicenna is ordinarily regarded as a neo-Platonist, in this we hear echoes of Aristotle's theory of the good, of the mean and of human flourishing. It is unsurprising then that Aquinas should discuss the metaphysics and ethics of diverse philosophers using reason alone.

critics of the natural law tradition

Although there is much classical support for the idea of a natural law universal and timeless, objective and rational, many argue that there is no such reality binding on all human beings at all times, as understood by Cicero and others. It is argued that morality and justice itself changes and progresses and is, in fact, socially constructed. The concept of natural rights, for example, is typically rejected by those who, like Jeremy Bentham in his *Anarchical Fallacies*, view them as "simple nonsense: natural and imprescriptible rights, rhetorical nonsense – nonsense upon stilts."[25] The assumption that there can be no eternal, universal or rational foundation for morality, never mind law, above that which is prescribed by human *fiat* underpins the atheism of Bentham, David Hume and many others. This scepticism about moral reality and rights is a challenge to the notion of a law that is universal and eternal, a principal tenet of Christian teaching on the subject of law revealed in both scripture and tradition.

Accordingly, some argue that, because both individuals and cultures differ in their approaches to ethical questions, there can be no timeless and universal truth: there can be no natural law. Some theological versions of individual conscience appear to require a similar conclusion. If each man is obliged to follow his own conscience and this can oblige conflicting acts at different times, then there can be no natural law that governs all men at all times.

There are numerous objections to this personal and cultural relativism, and an essay such as this one is no place to find a general account. But the fact that someone thinks X does not necessarily make X true. Individuals and cultures can be mistaken, misguided, conditioned, or coerced. The fact that an individual, or even a group of people, thinks child abuse, rape or genocide acceptable makes these activities no more right than they would be if there were no such views. There are also objections to the cultural relativist's attempt to reduce rightness to group beliefs or feelings about rightness. These relate to the arbitrariness of the standard to be used to determine, for example, which group's ideas represent those of the culture and which period of time is to be chosen as the test of rightness. If attitudes are in a state of flux, contradictory results flow. Equally, it cannot be assumed that the justice of the question is uncertain merely because attitudes can change.

Further, the very business of identifying the group whose ideas are to be determinative of the moral question at stake is itself ideologically driven. One group might reveal result 'p', while an alternative group might reveal result 'not-p'. Survey evidence about the morality of sex with infants derived from online paedophiles and sex criminals might be quite different from those got from a convent of Poor Clares.[26] Contradictory results flow if both are used, while choosing one group over another reveals more about the chooser's moral position than about the moral question at stake. What standard is to be used to determine a culture's beliefs is itself a problematic question.

There are also sound conceptual reasons to maintain the distinction between preferences and desires, on the one hand, and knowledge and reality, on the other. Preferences and desires are wholly determined by the subject whose desires they are, whereas knowledge and truth claims depend, at least in part, upon reality. Arguments from self-refutation also highlight the illogicality of statements of the form, "there are no rights and wrongs – but it is right to believe so." Christian philosophers have been foremost among those who have defended objective and universal values, and the natural law. According to traditional morality, we are able to know that God rules the entire universe by his providence. We can know the truth and seek the true and the good via reason.

natural law and human rights

The abandonment of a universal and rational foundation for law and ethics is itself subject to the challenge of gross injustice. The hypothesis that there is no rational foundation for positive law and that natural rights are "nonsense upon stilts" suggests it is possible that there is no irrationality and no injustice beyond that imposed by force. While this idea might appear progressive on paper, perhaps one of the greatest challenges to it is recent history. The Nuremberg Tribunals were set up shortly after the end of World War II with the main aim of seeing that justice was done in respect of perpetrators of war crimes, crimes of genocide, crimes against humanity and crimes against peace after the war. Those tried were often only obeying their own country's positive laws backed by the force of the state. The atrocities are a reminder that human *fiat* backed by force can arrive at diverse practical conclusions many of which are simply unjust, irrational, and contrary to the natural law ordained by God, man's eternal source and end.

The injustices of Stalinist Russia, Nazi Germany and numerous other regimes in the twentieth century have, in part, produced a body of international law designed to highlight certain fundamental human rights, or what might be interpreted as the natural moral law, to which all domestic positive law would be finally answerable. Whether positive international human rights law actually *amounts* to this or is instead, as some argue, an attempt to impose the interests of an elite upon domestic legislatures, is a separate question open to debate.[27] On the face of it, however, the drive to articulate laws against, for example, genocide, degrading and inhuman treatment, and other fundamental injustices, and insist that such prohibitions are not subject to cultural variation, emanates from the concern for a universal and unchangeable law written on the heart of man described earlier.

Of course, much could be said about the conceptual differences between human rights which are individualized and the natural law which is not (necessarily). Much has been written about whether human rights derive from an overly individualistic conception of justice. Some have argued that the notion of natural rights, fashioned by Locke and others, with the concern to elevate property rights, says more about the political underpinnings of capitalist systems than any concern for eternal, unchanging and universally enforceable norms.[28]

At a very simple level, however, there is a sense in which any classical natural law principle prohibiting the persecution of the innocent, for example, must be translatable into the individualist language of rights and duties. At this level, the contemporary language of rights must also fall into the natural law tradition with its concern for eternal and universal values, broadly understood. Christian thinkers have been prominent in the history of ideas about universal and unchanging human rights, the dignity of mankind, the protection of the innocent and procedural justice.

I have not tried here to argue that the law is more than a social construct. That task is beyond my remit. I have only attempted to show that if we want to hold on to the idea that certain activities and actions are timelessly unjust, whether genocide or child abuse or rape or slavery, then we have to jettison our view that both morality, and law in its fullest sense, i.e. that which binds the human conscience, is a mere human construct or convention. In other words, the *lex iniusta* principle had better make sense. Because human beings are capable of creating systems that impose injustice and support it with state sanction, anything, by definition, can purport to bind the human conscience and go by the name of law. Both morality and law properly understood, had better be more than that.

references

1 Sophocles, *Antigone*, trans. F. Storr (Cambridge, MA: Loeb Classical Library, 1912).

2 Marcus Tullius Cicero, *The Political Works of Marcus Tullius Cicero: Comprising his Treatise on the Commonwealth; and his Treatise on the Laws*. Translated from the original, with Dissertations and Notes in Two Volumes by Francis Barham, Esq. (London: Edmund Spettigue, 1841-42). Vol. 1. Laws I, p. 19.

3 Ibid. Vol. 1., Laws I, p. 42.

4 Ibid. Vol. 2., Laws II p. 10.

5 Ibid.

6 Plato, *The Apology*, The Dialogues of Plato, Volume 2, trans. Benjamin Jowett, 3rd Edition (Oxford: Oxford University Press, 1892) para. 57.

7 Ibid., para 68.

8 Psalm 148.6.

9 Proverbs 8.29.

10 Saint Thomas Aquinas, *The Summa Theologica of St. Thomas Aquinas* Second and Revised Edition, 1920. Literally translated by Fathers of the English Dominican Province. First Part of the Second Part.

11 John 1.1.

12 Saint Thomas Aquinas, op. cit., q. 94, a. 2.

13 Ibid, I, II q. 91, a3.

14 Ibid, I, II q. 95, a2.

15 Augustine *On the Free Choice of the Will*, trans. Thomas Williams (Indianapolis: Hackett Publishing, 1993) I, 6, see also *The City of God* Trans. Marcus Dods. From *Nicene and Post-Nicene Fathers*, First Series, Vol. 2. Edited by Philip Schaff. (Buffalo, NY: Christian Literature Publishing Co., 1887.)

16 Moses Maimonides, *The Eight Chapters of Maimonides on Ethics (Shemonah Perakim)* Translated by Joseph Gorfinkle, (New York, Columbia University Press, 1912).

17 Avicenna, 'On Love', trans. Emil Fackenheim *Medieval Studies*, 7 (1945), pp. 212-25.

18 Ibn Rushd, *On the Harmony of Religions and Philosophy*, trans. Mohammed Jamil-al-Rahmanin Arabic Kitabfasl al-maqal, with its appendix (Damina). Ibn Rushd, *The Philosophy and Theology of Averroes*, trans. Mohammed Jamil-al-Rahman (Baroda: A. G. Widgery, 1921), http://www.fordham.edu/halsall/source/1190averroes.asp

19 Maimonides, *Eight Chapters* op. cit., pp. 14, 56.

20 Moses Maimonides, *Mishneh Torah* I, Character Traits, 1, 4, in Isadore Twersky, *A Maimonides Reader* (Springfield, NJ: Behrman House, 1972).

21 Moses Maimonides, *Mishneh Torah*. I, Basic Principles, 4. 12 Ibid., p. 48.

22 Moses Maimonides, *Mishneh Torah*. I, Basic Principles, 4. 12.

23   Ibn Rushd, *On the Harmony of Religions and Philosophy*, translated by Mohammed Jamil-al-Rahman http://en.wikisource.org/wiki/On_the_Harmony_of_Religions_and_Philosophy.

24   Avicenna, 'On Love', op. cit., pp. 212-25.

25   Jeremy Bentham, 'Anarchical Fallacies' in *The Works of Jeremy Bentham* Vol II (Edinburgh: William Tait, 1843).

26   The possibility of producing desired results by way of selective survey evidence is far from mere fiction where the major financial interests of pornography are concerned: Judith Reisman, *Kinsey: Crimes & Consequences: The Red Queen and the Grand Scheme* (Arlington VA: The Institute for Media Education, 1998).

27   See, e.g., K. Mannheim, *Ideology and Utopia*, (New York: Harcourt, Brace and World 1936); Karl Marx and Friedrich Engels, *The German Ideology*, (Collected Works, Volume 6), (London: Lawrence and Wishart, 1976). S. Hymer, *The Multinational Corporation: A Radical Approach* (Cambridge: Cambridge University Press, 1979); Sypnowich, C. *The Concept of Socialist Law*, (Oxford: Clarendon Press. 1990)

28   Alasdair MacIntyre. *Marxism and Christianity*, (London: Duckworth, 1995) 2nd ed. cf First edition. See also Alasdair MacIntyre, *After Virtue*, (South Bend: University of Notre Dame Press, 1981) and the wealth of critical literature on this subject after MacIntyre.

is there a place and role for an established church in a liberal democratic state?

introduction

This essay sets out to explore whether there is a place and role for an established church in a modern liberal democratic state. It examines the possible answers to the question which it poses with regard to the position today of the Church of England. In doing so it seeks not to analyse and critique the various substantive and technical aspects of English Establishment,[1] but rather to unravel and evaluate its ideological underpinnings and practical rationales.

what is establishment/an established church?

In answering the question posed in the title the most obvious place to start is with a definition of what we mean by establishment or an established church. Unfortunately, it is far easier to pose the question than it is to provide a precise answer. Establishment is a distinctly local phenomenon, being the product of a range of political, social and historical factors which are unique to the experiences of the particular state in question.[2] Further, it is not simply a legal entity; it is also a political concept. It exists both in the law of that state, and in a web of theory and sentiment which have grown up in support of that law and interacted with its development in the course of history.[3]

At the most basic level, however, in any of the many forms which it can take, establishment can be seen to express a set of ties or relationships between the chosen church and the organs of the state; and between that church and the citizens of that state. These ties or relationships exist on the assumption that the state can and will take an interest in the affairs of the chosen church, and accord to it a special constitutional position, in return for the church's contribution to the formal and constitutional life of the state, and for the church's ministry to the nation (the citizens of the state) as a whole.[4] An established church is, then, one which occupies a special position in the law and constitution of the state as against other religious bodies, and one which owes an overt duty of spiritual care to all of the citizens of that state.

a clash of values and assumptions

From our definition of establishment, and of what constitutes an established church, it is already evident that these entities face significant challenges in the modern state. In the first place, the presumed value of a church which ministers to the nation as a whole is no longer axiomatic. Whatever one makes of the statistics on religious belief and affiliation it is undoubtedly the case that, in England at least, society is both far more pluralistic, and in some senses more secular, than was the case in previous centuries. In short, while many of its citizens continue to mark important life events according to the rites of the Church of England, and while many significant national events retain at their core a role for Anglican (and other) clergy, many of the state's citizens reject, or are at best largely indifferent to, the services of the established church. This uncomfortable reality calls into question the role of that church in the public forum. Yet, as Roger Trigg has noted:

> England may give the appearance of an increasingly secular country, in that religion plays less of a part in the lives of many than used to be the case. That can be exaggerated, but it does not answer the question as to whether a policy of aggressive secularism, driving religion out of public life, should be pursued.[5]

There is, however, a profound potential mismatch between establishment and the ethos and assumptions of a liberal democratic state. While establishment as practiced in England does not impinge, in law or the perception of those concerned, upon the rights to freedom of religion and from religion of its citizens, it is less easy to reconcile it with the principle of equality.[6] Further, and more fundamentally still, its very essence sits ill with the basic assumptions of Enlightenment liberalism. Establishment assumes that the state has a legitimate interest in religion, and that the church has a role to play in the public sphere. By contrast, at the heart of liberalism is a dichotomy between fact and value, or between the objective and subjective, and a corresponding dichotomy between what is public and what is private. Religion, which is assumed always to be subjective and irrational, is thus defined as belonging to the private sphere.[7] Religious belief is, therefore, something which is left at home when the believer steps across the threshold into the outside world.[8] Liberalism excludes religion from the public square, and, at the very least, appears to require the state to adopt a neutral stance in its dealings with and treatment of different religious bodies.[9]

There are many things at which one might cavil with regards to liberalism's schema for state dealings with religion. One might, for example, argue that state neutrality is nothing more than a myth, and that, if it exists at all, it may be as well served by allowing all religions a voice and role in the public square as it is by the exclusion of all.[10] The ability or willingness of individuals to relegate their religious beliefs to the private sphere, and the desirability of the exclusion of religious concerns and religiously motivated or derived arguments from public discourse and decision-making might also be called into question.[11]

Such arguments do not, however, address the propriety (or not) of the state's entry into a special relationship with one (or more) churches. Though, for example, English establishment long ago discarded all vestiges of the confessional state, and with it any state preference for the practice of a particular form of religion (see Julian Rivers' contribution in this volume), it might nevertheless be argued that establishment provides at least the appearance of the state's endorsement of a particular church's theological position. Yet not since the middle of the nineteenth century at the very latest has this been the case. It is pragmatism rather than theology that has rationalised and justified the Church of England's continued establishment. So, for example, in the nineteenth century many of its supporters defended its established status on the ground that it was, organisationally and practically, the religious body best able to fulfil a national mission.[12] More recently, albeit less stridently, the Wakeham Report on House of Lords reform justified *ex officio* seats for Anglican Bishops on the basis that this was a practical and readily available means of securing the representation of religious interests in the reformed second chamber.[13] Such pragmatism may be unsatisfactory, and even distasteful, but it has an undeniable place in the current canon of English constitutional development.

how (if at all) do the state and civil society benefit from an established church?

Moving on, to some extent at least, from the ideological arguments, and accepting establishment as, for the moment at least, a feature of the English constitutional landscape, the next obvious question is what benefit (if any) the state and civil society at large derive from the presence of an established church. It is to this question which we will now turn our attention.

Probably the most obvious rationale for establishment, at least historically, is that it reinforces the idea that the state is subject to a higher authority – that it is accountable to God, as well as the electorate, for its actions. The remnants of this unfashionable notion can be seen in the formula of "the Queen in Parliament under God", and in a somewhat muted reference made to it by the Royal Commission on House of Lords reform,[14] but it is clear that we have to look elsewhere if we wish to find meaningful ways of sustaining the place of establishment in the constitution today. In doing so, however, we find further difficulties for the traditional rationalisations of establishment.

In England, as in other liberal democracies, the assumption that there is a necessary link between religion and morality is challenged by undercurrents of moral relativism and enlightened cynicism.[15] This very assumption has, however, historically underpinned two of the most significant rationales for establishment and for the legitimacy of the state's interest in religious provision. As such, Anglican establishment theory has traditionally asserted the role of the Church of England as being to provide the state, which is seen as lacking such knowledge, with the moral knowledge to which it requires access in order properly to guide its actions.[16] Further, its adherents have traditionally defended establishment as providing the means by which the state could secure the moral and spiritual education of its citizens so that they were fitted to be worthy citizens of a state which was governed, as liberal democracies generally are, by law rather than by force.[17]

Most public policy-makers today, though they might willingly advocate the role of churches and other religious bodies in teaching citizenship, would shy away from defending establishment in these terms, and from articulating any necessary and inescapable link between law and morality, or even between moral sense and willingness to obey the law. So, too, is there an unwillingness to suggest that moral and philosophical knowledge and expertise are the sole preserve of religious persons and bodies.[18] Yet, as may be seen in the first White Paper and Wakeham Commission on House of Lords reform, there is clearly (in some quarters at least) a willingness to acknowledge the role that "moral, philosophical and theological considerations have to play in debating political and social issues."[19] Further, it appears from the recommendations of those reports that there is also some limited acceptance of the role that Bishops of the Church of England, together with other representatives of religion, might play as 'expert witnesses' in such matters.

The idea of the established Church of England as a sole or chief source of such 'expert witness' in the public forum is, to say the least, problematic. The Church of England has, however, evolved this role into one which, providing one is willing to countenance some place for religious views and arguments in the public forum, has a clear and defensible place in the modern state. It is a role, moreover, which the majority of other churches and faith groups appear to endorse. Put simply, the Church of England's constitutional position both signals that there is indeed a place for religion in the pubic square, and offers "an umbrella under which other religions can also shelter."[20] The Church of England acts as a stakeholder for those who believe that religion and religious views should be seen and heard in the public sphere, and also provides a conduit through which a diverse range of such views and concerns can be transmitted and represented in the machinery of the state.

It is in the idea of the established church as a stakeholder for the place of religion in the public sphere that we find probably the most important objective justification for the continuation of establishment today. It does not, however, answer the criticisms of those who continue to oppose the basic notion that religion and religiously motivated concerns and arguments have any legitimate role to play in the public square. To respond to these criticisms one must turn to one of the most basic and venerable assumptions of Anglican political theology. This rejects as being entirely fallacious Enlightenment liberalism's assumptions that there is a ready distinction between the spiritual and the secular aspects of life, and that the person of faith can meaningfully confine that faith to the private sphere. It asserts the unutterable damage done to believing citizens if their lives are pulled apart and fragmented by divisions and disagreements between the secular and the sacred, and if they are consistently forced to choose between competing obligations.[21]

In the modern context the argument to be derived from such theological contentions is not that religious considerations should be given primacy, or that they should trump other concerns. It must inevitably be recognised that there may be many situations in which the interests of wider society require both the state and persons of faith to make hard choices. From time to time tensions between secular and sacred obligations are unavoidable. Nevertheless, traditional Anglican establishment theory reminds us that there is a powerful argument against the marginalisation of religious voices, and of the religious or spiritual dimensions of the lives of individuals. It makes a convincing argument for their inclusion in the public square.

conclusion

It may be seen that, though many of the traditional rationalisations of establishment are admitted to be problematic – and even indefensible – the author advocates the continued role of an established church as recognising the value of religious voices and views in the public forum, and as asserting the value and significance of religious faith in the lives of many citizens. This essay, therefore, contests Enlightenment liberalism's determination to confine religion to the private sphere.

It must nevertheless be acknowledged that considerable difficulties remain, particularly when one looks at the position and current situation of the Church of England. One cannot escape, for example, the fact that the role which it plays as stakeholder and conduit for other religions is defensible only as a pragmatic and expedient constitutional compromise. Further, the problems faced by the Church of England as an institution cannot be ignored. The widening gulf between the Church of England and the majority of the citizens to which it is supposed to minister impacts upon the Church's confidence in that ministry. While reactions to this have varied, one consequence has arguably been an assertion of doctrinal identities and boundaries, a resulting loss of catholicity or breadth, and a tendency to turn inwards towards the needs and pre-occupations of a committed core of believers. Adrift upon a perceived sea of unbelief and indifference, many factions within the Church of England have sought both safety and a sense of spiritual identity and cohesion in increasingly sharply defined standards of belief and participation. These have, in turn, often served both to differentiate its members from wider society, and to place them in an oppositional stance as regards wider social trends. While this is understandable, and may in some senses even be defended as necessary to the Church of England's survival and integrity as a faith body,[22] it has arguably served further to undermine any notion of the Church of England's ministry to the nation as a whole, and has thereby potentially weakened the defensibility of its privileged position in the public forum.[23]

references

1   On the legal specifics of English Establishment See K. Medhurst and G. Moyser, *The Church and Politics in a Secular Age* (Oxford: Clarendon Press, 1988) chapters one and two; Bob Morris, "The Future of 'High' Establishment" *Ecclesiastical Law Journal* 13/3 (2011) pp. 260-273; Javier García Oliva, "Church, State and Establishment in the United Kingdom in the 21st Century: Anachronism or Idiocyncrasy?" *Public Law* [2010] pp. 482-504.

2   On this see J. Martinez-Torron, "Religious Liberty in European Jurisprudence" in M. Hill (ed.), *Religious Liberty and Human Rights* (Cardiff: University of Wales Press, 2002) pp. 99-127.

3   See P. M. H. Bell, *Disestablishment in Ireland and Wales* (London: S.P.C.K., 1969), Introduction.

4   P. Avis, *Church, State and Establishment* (London: S.P.C.K., 2000) pp. 15-16.

5   Roger Trigg, "Religion in the Public Forum" *Ecclesiastical Law Journal* 13/3 2011) pp. 274-286 at p. 279.

6   See Christopher McCrudden, "Religion, Human Rights, Equality and the Public Sphere" *Ecclesiastical Law Journal* 13/1 (2011) pp. 26-38; Bob Morris, "The Future of 'High' Establishment" *Ecclesiastical Law Journal* 13/3 (2011) pp. 260-273.

7   One might object to the apparent definition of rationality adopted here. On this point see D. L. D'Avray, *Rationalities in History: a Weberian Essay in Comparison* (Cambridge: Cambridge University Press, 2010).

8   See M. W. McConnell, "Religious Souls and the Body Politic" *The Public Interest*, [2004] pp. 126-142.

9   See T. Rowland, "The Liberal Doctrine of State Neutrality: a Taxonomy" *The University of Notre Dame Australia Law Review* 2 (2002) pp. 53-66.

10   See generally R. Ahdar and I. Leigh, *Religious Freedom in the Liberal State* (Oxford: Oxford University Press, 2005).

11   See Jonathan Chaplin, "The Place of Religious Arguments for Law Reform in a 'Secular State'" *Law and Justice – Christian Law Review* 18 (2009) pp. 18-35.

12   See e.g. S. T. Coleridge, *On the Constitution of Church and State According to the Idea of Each* (3rd Edition) (London: William Pickering, 1869) pp. 8-10; T. Arnold, *Fragments on Church and State* (London: B. Fellowes, 1845) pp. 55ff and F. D. Maurice, *The Kingdom of Christ or Hints to a Quaker Respecting the Principles, Constitution, and Ordinances of the Catholic Church* (3rd Edition) (London: Macmillan and Co., 1883), advertisement and introduction.

13   See Royal Commission on the Reform of the House of Lords, *A House for the Future* (Cm 4534, 2000) Para 15.8.

14   Ibid., Para 15.9.

15   For a discussion of the possible consequences of this see P. Weller, "Equity, Inclusivity and Participation in a Plural Society: Challenging the Establishment of the Church of England" in P. W. Edge and G. Harvey (eds.), *Law and Religion in Contemporary Society: Communities, Individualism, and the State* (Winchester: Ashgate Publishing, 2000) pp. 53-67.

16   See e.g. T. Arnold, *Fragment on the Church* (Second edition, London: B. Fellowes, 1845) pp. 9-13.

17   See e.g. W. E. Gladstone, *The State in its Relations to the Church* (4th Edition)(London: John Murray, 1841) pp. 60-63; R. Palmer, *A Defence of the Church of England against Disestablishment* (5th Edition)(London: Macmillan and Co., 1911) p. 73; S. T. Coleridge, *On the Constitution of Church and State*, op. cit. pp. 58, 76; S. L. Holland, *The National Church of a Democratic State* (London: Rivingtons, 1886) pp. 5-8.

18   See e.g. *A House for the Future* at Para 15.4.

19   White Paper, *The House of Lords Completing the Reform*, (Cm 5291, 2001) Para 83. See also *A House for the Future*, Paras 15.4 – 15.6 and Recommendation 107. For evidence of this one might point to notable contributions made by the Church of England to debates about social justice. See e.g. *Faith in the Nation: a Call to Action for Church and Nation* – the Report of the Archbishop of Canterbury's Commission on Urban Priority Areas (1985) (available at http://www.churchofengland.org/media/55076/faithinthecity.pdf) and Daniel Boffrey, "Archbishop Rowan Williams Backs Rebellion Against Coalition's Welfare Cuts," *The Guardian* 19 November 2011 (http://www.guardian.co.uk/politics/2011/nov/19/archbishop-rowan-williams-welfare-reforms).

20   Roger Trigg, "Religion in the Public Forum" *Ecclesiastical Law Journal* 13/3 (2011) pp. 274-286 at p. 284.

21   See e.g. T. Arnold, *Fragment on the Church*, p. 11 and F. D. Maurice, *The Kingdom of Christ* pp. 238-239. For a modern discussion of this question see M. W. McConnell, "Religious Souls and the Body Politic" *Public Interest* 155 (2004) pp. 126-142.

22   For an articulation of the reasons for this in the context of the nineteenth century see M. J. D. Roberts, *The Role of the Laity in the Church of England c1850 – 1885* (DPhil, Oxford, 1974).

23   On this point see e.g. P. Avis, *Church, State and Establishment* p. 16 and K. Medhurst, "The Church of England: a Progress Report" *Parliamentary Affairs*, (1999) pp. 275-290 at pp. 289-90.

is English law Christian?

introduction: why history is not enough

In some sense, the United Kingdom is still a Christian country. If pushed, a majority of people still associate themselves with Christianity. The Churches of England and Scotland are still 'established', albeit in ways largely symbolic and residual. We still celebrate the legacy of well-known Christian law reformers of earlier ages. We are proud of William Wilberforce, the seventh Earl of Shaftesbury, John Howard, Elizabeth Fry, and Seebohm Rowntree. Yet many people sense that public culture has shifted in the past decade or so away from Christianity. This intuition is reinforced by a handful of high profile cases in which Christians have been involved *as Christians* in litigation and have lost. Is English law becoming anti-Christian? In what sense is English law Christian anyway?

In 1989, on his retirement as President of the Lawyers' Christian Fellowship, Lord Denning (Master of the Rolls 1962-1981) published a pamphlet in which he argued that English law had been beneficially affected by Christianity in a number of ways.[1] These included a belief in the importance of truth, requirements of good faith in statutory interpretation and contractual obligations, the development of the law of negligence, basic presuppositions of criminal law (such as the requirement to demonstrate that the accused had a 'guilty mind'), the principle of government under law, the rise of social welfare legislation, and the centrality of a Christian conception of marriage.

It would be easy to add to this list. Modern commitments to political liberty and equality within the law emerged out of debates which were internal to Christianity; debates which were catalysed by the inescapably radical liberty and equality exemplified by Jesus and his disciples.[2] Jesus is the model of the accountable public servant, using power for the good of others and conscious of his answerability to a higher tribunal. English nationhood owes more than a little to the example of Israel.[3] Christianity also reinforced a commitment to authority, order and the rule of law.

However, arguments such as these are inadequate in themselves. Some of Denning's examples are easy to dismiss as mere rhetorical flourishes. It is hard to believe that when Lord Atkin made reference to the parable of the Good Samaritan in his judgment in

Donoghue v Stevenson,[4] the teaching of Jesus was doing any serious substantive work. The general principle of civil liability for negligently caused harm may well be compatible with Christianity, but it is hardly a distinctive contribution of Christianity to the history of legal ideas. Even where we can show a causal connection in the history of ideas, history is not enough. It is true that modern criminal law requires the law to treat the accused as a responsible agent: criminality requires moral culpability. Just because this derives historically from a Christian concern with sin, guilt and divine judgment, it does not follow that such a conception is distinctively Christian. It may be true that liberty, equality, accountability, procedural fairness, the rule of law all have Christian roots, but more needs to be shown. English law may be *compatible* with Christianity; it may even in some respects be historically *derived* from Christianity, but for the most part it seems not to require or predispose one to Christian belief and practice. Plenty of non-Christians share such commitments. English law may be Christian in origin, but is it distinctively Christian today?

abandoning coercive Christianity

Historically, English law has been used to coerce Christian belief and practice in quite direct ways.[5] It is important to note that this was closely connected with the rise of modernity and features such as the sovereign European state aligned to one or another Christian denomination. For about a century and a half (1535-1688), English public law sought to secure the exclusive dominance of a single church. Thereafter, a process of expanding toleration saw Trinitarian Protestants, Unitarians, Roman Catholics and Jews brought within the law, until around the mid-nineteenth century, when the law stopped thinking in terms of specific religions.[6] However, until about the end of the nineteenth century it was still possible to assert that it was the policy of English common law to penalise opposition to Christianity. As late as 1867 the courts could hold that a contract to let a room to the Secular Society for the purposes of a lecture impugning the character and teachings of Jesus Christ was invalid.[7] Only in 1883 did it become clear that one could attack the fundamentals of Christianity without landing oneself with a blasphemy prosecution.[8] The nails in the coffin of the view that the law directly promotes Christianity were hammered in by the House of Lords in two cases, in 1917 and 1919. In the first, the House of Lords held that opposition to Christianity was not contrary to the policy of the law.[9] Indeed, many of their lordships expressed astonishment that anyone could still maintain such an antiquated view. In the second, it was confirmed that the law knows no doctrine of superstitious uses. In other words, there are no unlawful religions for the purposes of charity law.[10] The last whisper of the direct enforcement of Christian orthodoxy by the law was finally removed when the common law of blasphemy was abolished in 2008.[11]

Having abandoned the enforcement of doctrinal orthodoxy, English law also abandoned the enforcement of Christian virtue. In (very) long-term historical perspective, the policing of 'sin' was first of all a responsibility of ecclesiastical courts. The long-term effect of the Reformation was both to trigger the decline of ecclesiastical courts and to 'moralise' the common law. From a European comparative perspective, the English ecclesiastical courts survived a remarkably long time. But their attempts to punish sins (such as profanity, drunkenness and fornication) had already died out in the early eighteenth century, along with their attempts to punish non-attendance at church.[12] Concern about the lax state of public morals led in time to a more systematic use of secular law to enforce Christian ethics. Whereas the medieval Christian polity had known a multiplicity of jurisdictions, royal, mercantile, local and ecclesiastical, the Victorian conception of a 'Christian nation' conceived of a unitary system of law under government thoroughly imbued with Christian ethics. It was the 1960s which saw the final collapse of this model. A wave of liberalising legislation systematically detached the content of law from traditional Christian understandings of sin. Suicide, abortion, gambling, obscenity, divorce, homosexuality, and Sunday recreation all became subject to a relaxation of laws.

So English law is not Christian in the sense of directly promoting Christian doctrine or worship, nor does it oppose everything Christianity treats as sinful or immoral. And many, perhaps most, Christians would support these instances of law's retrenchment. The coercive force of the law should not be used to compel people to enter the Kingdom of God, nor is it wise for Government to seek to suppress every vice known to humankind. Worries about too close an alignment between the fundamentally coercive state and the church whose mission is to proclaim a gospel of free grace and personal transformation were what powered Christian nonconformist Protestants to challenge and substantially change the nature of Anglican establishment.[13] The ways in which English law is no longer Christian are not obviously incompatible with a Christian understanding of the proper purpose of law.

Christianity and law: relating the two

This leaves us with a puzzle. If it is not Christian to use law to enforce Christian belief and behaviour, in what sense can law be Christian? The contrast with Islam and Judaism is instructive at this point. Islam and Judaism came to be expressed historically as complete and distinctive legal traditions.[14] They manifested themselves as the law of an entire community organised around those faiths. So it makes sense to talk of Islamic or Jewish criminal law, family law, property law, law of contracts, charitable foundations and so on. Of course, these religions themselves contain a range of views on the proper place and content of law. Not only are there different schools of Islamic jurisprudence, but modern day

Islamic majority countries range from the rigorously traditional (e.g. Iran) to the substantially secular (e.g. Turkey). The rise of the modern state has produced major challenges for both these religious traditions, and as a result the place of religion in the law of such countries can be highly contested. Nevertheless, the historic experience of a complete community expressing its faith in God by living under its own law makes it relatively meaningful to ask, for example, how Jewish the modern law of Israel is, or how Islamic the law of Egypt.

The political and legal implications of Christianity have been quite different.[15] Throughout its history, Christianity has been characterised in some form or another by what the political theologian Oliver O'Donovan calls 'the doctrine of the two'.[16] Under God, there are two authorities on earth, not one, and they are church and government. The sphere of church is characterised by salvific grace, by individual commitment, by freedom – so much so that the very concept of law might be out of place in the church (although Christian ecclesiological traditions vary considerably on that particular question). The sphere of government is characterised by judgment and coercion in the service of goods common to all of humankind. The tasks of government may be considered primarily in terms of restraining evil, or of coordinating human action in pursuit of the common good (Christian political traditions vary considerably on *that* question too).[17] In practice, what we put in the two spheres of church and government, and their mutual relationship to each other, has always shifted.[18] Only in the 1860s did the English ecclesiastical courts lose their general jurisdiction over family law, wills, defamation and some residual criminal offences. And we should not forget that it was only in the first half of the twentieth century that the balance of welfare functions in the relief of poverty, sickness, infirmity and the provision of education shifted from church to state.

The dualism of Christian political theory is multilayered. It plays out not only as a contrast between institutions such as 'church' and 'state', but also between different ways of knowing and acting, between 'grace' and 'nature', between 'order' and 'freedom', between the present age and the age to come. And it raises fundamental questions about the extent to which the one can and should engage with and penetrate the other. This gives rise to a wide range of models for the interaction between Christianity and law.[19] So in contrast to Islam or Judaism, the political and legal heritage of Christianity is not a single tradition of customary law with central themes and variations. It is not about law being more or less Christian. Rather, Christianity sets up substantial tensions, the terms of which are subject to continual renegotiation.

It follows that the relationship between the law and Christianity is inextricably bound up with the history of secularisation.[20] Secularisation can mean a number of things, but two of its key senses are: (1) the process of social structural differentiation; and (2) the construction of religion as a matter of personal choice and commitment. Both of these senses flow from

Christianity. In the first sense, the ancient distinction between church and government multiplied after the Reformation to produce other social institutions such as schools and hospitals, which, while still imbued with a Christian spirit, were organisationally relatively independent of both church and government. In the second sense, Christianity's emphasis on personal faith in God as opposed to collective norms of right worship and right living led to the idea that this is characteristic of religion in general.

This means that the law can still be 'Christian' even where it has ceased to be 'expressly Christian'. The paradox is only apparent, because the law reflects shifts in judgment about its proper use from a Christian perspective. Perhaps the position could be put like this: English law is Christian in the sense that for the most part it is consistent with a Christian view of the proper purpose and content of secular law. It represents a possible expression of the 'doctrine of the two'. This does not mean that all Christians agree with all of it; rather, disagreements about what the law should be are not clearly disagreements between Christians and non-Christians.

could English law cease to be Christian?

The Christian tensions between church and state, between freedom and order, between grace and nature, the future and the present are not like the 'fundamental contradictions' of Critical Legal Studies.[21] They do not admit of every possible outcome. Perhaps it is best to think of the range of options as two circles which can overlap to a greater or lesser extent. We can characterise liberal modernity as a particularly rigorous expression of Christianity's 'doctrine of the two' in which a clean line is drawn between government on the basis of natural law and natural rights universally conceived and church as a voluntary association of believers.[22]

This Christian natural law tradition arguably reached its fulfilment in the Universal Declaration of Human Rights and the mid-twentieth century human rights movement more generally. Fascism and communism were both correctly seen as hostile to the basic Christian framework, one on account of its failure to respect the equal dignity of all human beings, the other on account of excessive state authority and restrictions on the freedom of the church. The Universal Declaration is founded on a Christian understanding of human dignity which is given shape by the purposes of God for humankind. It assumes a value-laden understanding of what is 'natural' for human beings. In its protection of civil liberty alongside civil, political, economic, social and cultural rights, the Universal Declaration also assumes the limitations of state power in favour of church-like associations of truth, beauty and goodness.[23]

If the early twentieth century threats to this Christian understanding of human dignity and human flourishing came from communism and fascism, it is possible that the twenty-first century threat arises from an alternative post-modern understanding of human dignity allied to new intrusive forms of state regulation. This view supposes that our basic moral worth as human beings inheres in our being self-creating beings, with no divine pattern. We are Nietzschean 'works of art' who fashion ourselves as we please. Thus our bodies are what we make of them, religion is whatever we believe it to be (if anything); gender, sexuality and family is whatever we want of it, and in our chosen form of death we write the final chapter in our own stories. This is what gives us dignity, and a commitment to equal dignity requires us to recognise and respect each person's self-created identity and lifestyle. It becomes a social offence to speak against it, or to suggest that fulfilment may be found instead in submission to any externally-grounded ethic. This vision of human dignity is anti-Christian, because it is essentially idolatrous. It rejects the very idea of a pattern for human fulfilment set by a divine creator and worships the individual human (self-)creator instead.

As well as a possible shift in the underlying conception of human dignity, there also seems to be a new political absolutism influencing the law. The rhetoric of equal respect – if not the law itself – is making it harder to have a public debate about the requirements of the common good, particularly in areas of sexual ethics, family life, medical law and bioethics. The working assumption is that there is no common good for which we could jointly search. There are also developments that are beginning to restrict the autonomy of the church in its internal affairs and external mission.[24] The oversight of secular courts, even if it is still relatively benign, no longer leaves churches entirely free to organise themselves in matters of doctrine, worship, discipline and government. An historic commitment to conscience seems to be faltering, and instead replaced by an obligation to adhere to the social ethic imposed by law. The terms of collaboration between the state and religious bodies in education and social welfare are increasingly dictated by the state, rather than being negotiated between partners conceived of as equals, and they are increasingly difficult to comply with.

However, even if we accept that a legal system based on self-constructed 'dignity' and an intrusive state is anti-Christian, the hypothesis that this is taking place within English law is undoubtedly contentious. The line is very fine between postmodern dignity and a radical interpretation of Protestant and Enlightenment commitments to individual moral integrity, kept firmly inside boundaries of objective other-regarding morality.[25] State oversight of the 'external' or 'temporal' aspects of church life is hardly a novelty. Perhaps only with hindsight will we be able to see whether such a tectonic shift is taking place.

the example of same-sex marriage

The Government's proposal to allow two people of the same sex to marry exemplifies very well the difficulties of reading the times.[26] As Lord Denning suggested, there can be no doubt that the law of marriage and family has historically been significantly influenced by Christian ethics. In many detailed ways one can still trace the direct impact of Christian teaching and canon law. At the same time, secular family law has departed in various ways from historic Christian teaching, not least in its acceptance of divorce. However, this is still compatible with a recognisably Christian view in which the secular law sustains a basic, 'natural' and universal framework of rights, responsive to human needs and weaknesses, while the Church is free to teach a higher ideal, to which Christians and others can aspire. The law still represents coordination between nature/State and grace/Church, in which the latter fulfils and enhances the former.

The Government's proposals clearly depart from an historic Christian understanding of the 'natural' relationship of marriage, effectively rejecting it as culturally constructed and an unjust imposition of 'Christian' views on those with a different understanding of appropriate sexual relationships. Even if one does not accept a revisionist Christian affirmation of same-sex relationships, one could see this merely as a further 'thinning' of an indefensibly thick and value-laden conception of the natural. After all, humankind has known considerable diversity in this area. Yet the Government's proposals are not defended by reference to any new universal conception of human flourishing. Rather, the principal justification is based on 'equality and fairness', which can only mean respect for each individual's conception of what marriage is. In this, there is more than a hint of postmodern dignity at work.

Again, in itself, this need not be oppressive. It is possible that one effect of the proposed changes would be to move to a system common in continental Europe in which the role of the state and the role of religious bodies are more clearly distinct. The state recognises and regulates a range of personal and domestic arrangements – which after all emerge primarily as a matter of social fact. Some of these arrangements some Christians may well deem inappropriate, but religious bodies are free to discipline and exclude on one hand, and to celebrate and bless on the other, in accordance with their own ethos and law. This classic Christian solution to the problem of diversity is gestured at by the Government in its references to 'civil' and 'religious' marriage.

But will postmodern dignity be combined with a willingness to use state power through law to secure uniform acceptance? After all, given the existence of civil partnership, the proposal is primarily about controlling discourse, not conferring rights. It is likely that schools may be obliged to promote the new view of marriage, and unclear whether there will be rights of conscientious objection, collective or individual.[27] Churches have been promised freedom of action in respect of teaching and practice, but this must now be read in a context of recent non-discrimination norms which may not tailor exceptions to every circumstance of their wider activity in society, still less that of individual Christians.

Thus it is hard to see the issue of same-sex marriage as a debate internal to Christianity about the natural in human flourishing, and the proper role of the state in promoting universal human goods. We should take seriously the possibility that it represents instead a paradigm shift towards a denial of the 'natural' in any normatively charged sense and to the universal mandate of the state to protect each individual in his or her vulnerable self-construction. If this is the better reading of the proposal, it is hard to see it as falling within the range of Christian possibility.

So a full answer to the question posed in this chapter runs as follows: English Law is Christian in the sense that it largely reflects the possible outcome of debates within Christianity about the proper limited purpose and content of secular law, but it may be departing from Christianity in its flirtation with an idolatrous (self-worshipping) conception of human dignity and its willingness to use the power of the law to promote that conception across the whole of society. The irony is that Christianity was born 2,000 years ago into a world not so very different in that respect.

references

1   The Rt. Hon. Lord Denning, *The Influence of Religion on Law* (Lawyers' Christian Fellowship, 1989).

2   Nick Spencer, *Freedom and Order: The Bible and British Politics* (London: Hodder & Stoughton, 2011).

3   Adrian Hastings, *The Construction of Nationhood* (Cambridge: CUP, 1997).

4   *Donoghue v Stevenson* [1932] A.C. 562.

5   For a brief review of the history of the relationship between law and religion in England, see Julian Rivers, *The Law of Organized Religions: Between Establishment and Secularism* (Oxford: Oxford University Press, 2010), ch. 1.

6   The Places of Worship Registration Act 1855 was the key point of transition.

7   *Cowan v Milbourne* (1867) L.R. 2 Ex. 230.

8   *R v Ramsey and Foote* (1883) 15 Cox CC 231.

9   *Bowman v Secular Society* [1917] A.C. 406.

10   *Bourn v Keane* [1919] A.C. 815. The question of what counted as publicly beneficial 'religion' arguably remained influenced by Protestant Christian concerns.

11   Russell Sandberg and Norman Doe, 'The strange death of blasphemy' *Modern Law Review* 71/6 (2008) p. 971.

12   R.B. Outhwaite, *The Rise and Fall of the English Ecclesiastical Courts, 1500-1860* (Cambridge: Cambridge University Press, 2006).

13   Timothy Larsen, *Friends of Religious Equality: Non-conformist politics in mid-Victorian England* (The Boydell Press, 1999).

14   H. Patrick Glenn, *Legal Traditions of the World*, 2nd edn. (Oxford: Oxford University Press, 2004).

15   John Witte, Jr. and Frank S. Alexander, *Christianity and Law: An Introduction* (Cambridge: Cambridge University Press, 2008).

16   Oliver O'Donovan, *The Desire of the Nations: Rediscovering the Roots of Political Theory* (Cambridge: Cambridge University Press, 1996).

17   See, e.g., Nick Spencer and Jonathan Chaplin (eds.), *God and Government* (SPCK, 2008); Michael Cromartie (ed.), *A Preserving Grace: Protestants, Catholics and Natural Law* (Grand Rapids: Eerdmans, 1997); Stephen J. Grabill, *Rediscovering the Natural Law in Reformed Theological Ethics* (Grand Rapids: Eerdmans, 2006).

18   See the magisterial treatment by Harold J. Berman, *Law and Revolution*, 2 vols. (Cambridge, Mass.: Harvard University Press, 1983 and 2003).

19   For a classic typology, see H. Richard Niebuhr, *Christ and Culture* (New York: Harper Torchbooks, 1951). For an application to legal thought, see Michael McConnell, Robert F. Cochrane, Jr. and Angela C. Carmella, *Christian Perspectives on Legal Thought* (New Haven: Yale University Press, 2001). For an integrated application to current legal and political controversies, see D. A. Carson, *Christ and Culture Revisited* (Nottingham: Apollos, 2008).

20   Charles Taylor, *A Secular Age* (Cambridge, Mass.: Belknap Press, 2007).

21   Duncan Kennedy, 'Form and Substance in Private Law Adjudication' *Harvard Law Review* 89 (1976) 1685; id., 'The Structure of Blackstone's Commentaries' *Buffalo Law Review* (1979) 205.

22   John Locke gave this version of Christian political thought its classic expression (see Jeremy Waldron, *God, Locke and Equality: Christian Foundations in Locke's Political Thought* (Cambridge: Cambridge University Press, 2002)), and the United States is its most faithful instantiation.

23   See Julian Rivers, 'Liberal Constitutionalism and Christian Political Thought' in Paul Beaumont (ed.), *Christian Perspectives on the Limits of Law* (Carlisle: Paternoster Press, 2002).

24   Julian Rivers, 'The Secularisation of the British Constitution' *Ecclesiastical Law Journal* 14 (2012) (forthcoming).

25   This is well exemplified by Ronald Dworkin's consistent defence of a 'right to moral independence' in matters of ethics (i.e. in questions of how we ought to live) as opposed to morality which sets objective limits on how we treat each other. See, most recently, *Justice for Hedgehogs* (Cambridge, Mass.: Belknap Press, 2011). For the close connection with Nietzsche, see pp. 258-260.

26   Government Equalities Office, *Equal civil marriage: a consultation* (March, 2012).

27   The Education Act 1996, s. 403, provides among other things that when sex education is given to children at maintained schools they learn 'the nature of marriage and its importance for family life and the bringing up of children'.

does the law need a moral basis?

introduction

The Food Protection (Emergency Prohibitions) (Amnesic Shellfish Poisoning) (West Coast) (No. 10) (Scotland) Order 2005 is a brilliant example of the extent to which contemporary law in Britain appears technical and obscure, far removed from any discernable connection with morality. It is, however, one thing to say that law is not identical to morality, and quite another to deny that there is any relationship at all between law and morality.

law is not identical to morality

The recognition that law is not identical to morality, that that which can be and should be subject to public regulation and resolution is not coextensive with that which is morally wrong, is an old one. Even when the Church operated its own court system in the Middle Ages, it recognised that there was a distinction between crime and sin and that there were some moral wrongs for which people were answerable only to God.

questions of the right and the good

Ancient and mediaeval thought, by and large, considered that the answers to two big philosophical questions – 'What makes for a good human life?' and 'How would it be right for me to treat other people?' – went together. In other words, the questions of the Good and the Right were interconnected. John Locke argued that the two could be separated. We disagree with one another about what makes for a good human life and those disagreements show no sign of being resolved any time soon. Nonetheless, Locke suggested, we can agree with one another about how we should treat one another because we can all recognise and agree to respect each other's natural rights. Locke gives us the intellectual tool-kit which leads to the assertions today: 'it's my life and none of your business' and 'it's my right'.

Locke's approach tends to reduce the question of what makes for a good human life to a matter of individual taste. This finds its apogee in the argument between Bentham and J.S. Mill about whether "push-pin is as good as poetry".[1] For Bentham, and those libertarians and utilitarians who follow him on this point, each of us is free to decide for ourselves what we like and what we dislike, what increases or decreases our well-being, and no-one else has any right to criticise us, *unless* what we are doing decreases the well-being of others.

This way of thinking about the right and the good gives rise to one of those mental images of the role of government which many people today find intuitively appealing: the idea of the neutral public square. This is the picture of life as a competition, in which each of us wants to pursue the things that we think will make us happy, and the job of the government, the role of the law, is to act as an impartial umpire, making sure that the competition remains free and fair. So the law makes no judgments about the relative merits of loud rock music and enjoying a quiet Sunday afternoon walk, but provides regulations which make both possible within limits.

It is this idea of the law as neutral which gives rise to the popular misconception that the law is a-moral. This is, however, a mistake, even in the terms of those theorists who defend the idea that the law is or should be neutral between different conceptions of the Good.

Bentham founded his philosophy of Utilitarianism upon the idea that the right thing to do is the thing which maximises overall well-being. This idea is called the Utility Principle.

Benthamite Utilitarianism leads to the conclusion that law should be neutral between people's differing conceptions of the good. However, Benthamite Utilitarianism insists that this neutrality is right. In other words, even if people should be allowed to make their own minds up about what is good, Benthamite Utilitarianism offers a public answer to the question: what is right, what is the right way to treat other people? Moreover, Benthamite Utilitarianism has a meta-theory of the good. Benthamite Utilitarianism tells us that what is good for people is whatever increases their well-being without disproportionately decreasing the well-being of others. For Benthamite Utilitarianism, law does need a moral basis and that moral basis is provided by the 'Utility Principle' which tells us that *the right thing to do* is the thing which maximises overall well-being.

It's not just Benthamite Utilitarianism that supports the idea that we can answer the question of how it is right to treat other people without agreeing about what is good for people. John Rawls, probably the most influential political philosopher of the last generation, developed his *Theory of Justice* based on the ideas of John Locke and Immanuel Kant.[2] Rawls tells us that we can agree on an answer to the question of how it is right to treat others even if we disagree about what makes for a good human life.

Ronald Dworkin also claims that liberal states must "be neutral on what might be called the question of the good life [and thus] political decisions must be, so far as possible, independent of any particular conception of the good life, or of what gives value to life."[3] But, for him, this is fully compatible with public liberal morality "taking rights seriously".

For Bentham, Rawls, Dworkin and their followers, law is not a-moral; it does not fall outside the scope of morality and is not neutral with regards to all moral questions. Rather, these thinkers argue that law should be neutral with regards to *some* moral questions. Law should not express definitive views on what constitutes a good human life, but it should adopt this stance for good moral reasons based on the answers to the question of how it is right for us to treat one another.

Let me illustrate the distinction. The thinkers discussed above would all agree that law should not be neutral on questions like murder and theft. Whatever good you want to pursue in life, they presume that you want to be protected against being murdered and having your belongings stolen. However, beyond that, people should be left to work out for themselves what makes for a good life and should be left to get on with living it.

So, to sum up where we have got to so far: across a wide range of liberal thinkers, there is agreement that law should not express definitive views about what constitutes a good life, but that this is because of moral reasons about how it is right for us to treat one another.

Why, then, is there a popular conception that law does not need a moral basis? I want to suggest that there are three reasons for this. First, because we are taught to think of law and morality as two entirely separate categories; second, because we slip easily from recognising the fact of moral disagreement into thinking that there are no right answers to moral questions; and third, because of scepticism about the laws made as a result of our democratic processes.

legal positivism: treating law and morality as separate categories

For centuries in the West, the dominant family of legal theories was Natural Law. According to Natural Law theories, human law is a specification and an application of moral principles to be found within nature. Immoral laws were, therefore, not law, or were defective as law.

In the twentieth century, Natural Law was displaced by Legal Positivism. Advocates of Legal Positivism, such as Hans Kelsen and H. L. A. Hart, argued that the existence of a law is one thing, and the morality of a law is quite another. Legal Positivism maintains that we think more clearly about law when we treat the question of a law's morality as an entirely extrinsic question to the question of whether what we are dealing with is a law in the first place or not.

If that was all that Legal Positivism implied, it would look as if the argument between Legal Positivism and Natural Law was a scholastic dispute. However, it is easy to slip from thinking that the morality of a law is a question extrinsic to the nature of law as such to thinking that this question does not need to be asked at all. In the US at the turn of twentieth century, judges claimed that the interpretation of statutes and legal precedents was purely a formal exercise. A judge deciding a case was not making a moral decision but was merely applying a rule, in the same way that one would apply a rule of grammar.

After the Second World War, Gustav Radbruch, who had been a legal positivist between the two World Wars, suggested that legal positivist ideas allowed German lawyers and judges to apply Nazi laws without ever asking themselves whether the laws which they were applying were moral or immoral. He argued that Natural Law would have prevented this because of its insistence that human laws are derived from morality and do not create it.

Quite apart from the question of whether Radbruch's criticism of the German legal professions under Nazi Germany is justified, there is a major danger that the idea that law and the morality of law are two wholly different things reduces practitioners of law to mere technicians. And when lawyers are nothing more than technicians then the rest of society is in trouble, as the law then becomes nothing more than a tool, a weapon, to be wielded in the interests of lawyers and their clients, regardless of the cost to society as a whole.

Thinking about law as nothing more than a technique also has other pernicious effects. In the 1980s the UK had relatively few express rules governing financial services activities. Today, we have the misnamed FSA 'Handbook', which runs to thousands and thousands of pages. Despite that, we have seen a major financial crisis which exposed immoral and reckless behaviour on a grand scale in the financial system. Even before the credit crisis, Alistair Alcock criticised the increasing emphasis on rules as meaning that whereas in the 1980s people in the financial services sector asked themselves whether what they were doing was right, in the 1990s they asked themselves whether what they were doing was within the rules. Many of the accounting manoeuvres carried out in the WorldCom scandal were within the letter of American accounting rules, but their cumulative effect was to present a picture of the company's finances which was misleading to the tune of $9bn!

We will treat each other rightly only if we focus our attention on whether we are acting in ways which are honest, just and fair, and not if we are constantly looking for legal loopholes as ways of avoiding our responsibilities. A purely technical approach to rule-following is a bad way of obeying the law and an even worse way of trying to achieve justice.

scepticism about right answers to moral questions

It is too simplistic to conclude that Legal Positivism inevitably leads to indifference to the morality of law. However, the rise of Legal Positivism was associated with the rise of the philosophy of Logical Positivism and with a general and increasing scepticism amongst philosophers about the possibility of ever finding right answers to moral questions.

Logical Positivism, as a philosophical position, says that the only meaningful statements relate to matters of fact and the analytical truths of logic and mathematics. Claims about morality and metaphysics are not either true or false, they are simply meaningless. Logical Positivism reduces the sources of our ethical, political and legal standards to "exercises of the will of charismatic individuals or power-seeking groups".[4] The questions of the right and the good are therefore not just questions on which people disagree as to the correct answers. There are no correct answers because these questions are nonsense.

Part of the reason that we find it so difficult to make sense of moral questions, let alone to begin to work out how we might find widely accepted answers to them, is that we in the West have deprived ourselves of the tools of reasoning which we need to conduct moral argument. Immanuel Kant bears a large share of the responsibility for this.[5] On many pressing issues, our public debates take place within a set of assumptions drawn from Kant. It is Kant who gives us the idea that life divides into two compartments: a public compartment where we discuss things with one another on the basis of reason and a private compartment where reason has nothing to say. And it is Kant who establishes the modern trade-off regarding religion: no religion will be subjected to question on the grounds of its rationality provided that religions stay out of the public square. Even if most people today do not accept the Logical Positivist view that all moral questions fall into the private compartment where reason has nothing to say, the reasons which are currently acceptable in public discourse are so few and so thin that we cannot use them to build or to sustain agreement.

scepticism about the laws made as a result of our democratic processes

American legal theorists worry today about instrumental law, about law viewed purely as a means to an end. Brian Tamanaha argues that such an account of law has become dominant in the United States of America to the point where it is taken for granted that "law [is] an instrument of power to advance [people's] personal interests or the interests or policies of the individuals or groups they support."[6]

The particular danger in a democracy dominated by a small number of tightly disciplined political parties is that the parties become vehicles for the promotion of the interests of limited groups within society. Three things seem to dominate the concerns of political parties in election years: (1) how to attract the funds they need to campaign; (2) how to satisfy the aspirations of their core supporters; and (3) how to win the marginal seats they need to win in order to obtain victory.

As a result, politics is less a reasoned debate about what is in the interest of the public as a whole and instead a see-saw contest in which first one group in society and then another gains the upper hand and attempts to exploit the resources of the nation for its own benefit.

The problem with this is the opposite of the problem which worried Gustav Radbruch. Whereas he was concerned that legal positivism could lead to us blindly following whatever laws are made by those in power, scepticism about whether the laws being made are anything more than expressions of sectional interests leads us to see no reason whatsoever to regard those laws as morally binding upon us. The result, put bluntly, is the breakdown in law and order.

How, then, do we recover a moral basis for law whilst continuing to recognise that there is a difference between law and morality?

recovering the moral basis for law

understanding law as a sub-category of morality

Under the continuing influence of Legal Positivism today, many legal theorists still think of morality as one category and law as another, completely separate, category. This is a conceptual error.

Law is a sub-category of morality, that sub-category which relates to the morally based rules which we have adopted in order to regulate our life together as a political community. As Joseph Raz has written, "legal reasoning is an instance of moral reasoning. Legal doctrines are justified only if they are morally justified, and they should be followed only if it is morally right to follow them."[7]

Michael Sandel, whose celebrated Harvard lectures on justice were televised on BBC4, argues that the ideal of "liberal neutrality", which has dominated modern law and jurisprudence for decades – namely that we should never "bring moral or religious convictions to bear in public discourse about justice and rights"– is an impossibility. The reason is that:

> Justice is inescapably judgmental. Whether we're arguing about financial bailouts…, surrogate motherhood or same-sex marriage, affirmative action or… CEO pay…questions of justice are bound up with competing notions of honour and virtue, pride and recognition. Justice is not only about the right way to distribute things. It is also about the right way to value things.[8]

What is significant is that Sandel's examples are not just about private choices; they are about questions of what the law should and should not permit. They are about how the law reflects our public morality.

We need to return to teaching law as a branch of morality. We need to teach not just what the rules are but also about the moral vision to which the rules give expression. In subjects like banking law, the one I teach, it is far more important to teach students why we regulate banks and what sorts of behaviour we seek to promote and to penalise than it is to lose them in the forest of the detailed regulations about the level of capital which banks should hold and how that should be calculated. Indeed, I would argue that the only way to enable those students to find their way through that forest is to identify the moral signposts which lie behind the legislation.

a renewed commitment to the possibility of right answers to moral questions

Second, we need a renewed commitment to the possibility of right answers to moral questions. Nobody really believes that there are no right answers to any moral questions. Almost everybody in the UK today believes that sex with children, murder and gross forms of racism are wrong.

And yet, neither the idea of the neutral public square nor the way in which issues are aired today encourages us to work moral issues through to a reasoned conclusion. The standard of public debate about moral questions is extremely poor. Whether it is politicians shouting at one another in the House of Commons or people screaming at one another on the Jeremy Kyle show, we seem to be presented with a stand-up row far more often than we are ever treated to a sensible discussion.

Somehow or other, we need to recover a space where we can have proper discussions about those things which are good and commendable, which we as a society wish to promote.

This is not to claim that there are uniquely and verifiably correct solutions to all moral questions, still less that there are uniquely correct laws which ought to be introduced to address all moral problems. What is imperative, however, is a return to objective morality as the framework within which legislation is formulated and case-law is made.

a renewed insistence on the common good

If a sceptical view of law today sees politics as merely the will-to-power of different sections of society, we need a renewed vision of government as being in the interests of society as a whole, of government as working for the common good.

Although one of the most important aspects of human dignity is our freedom to be able to make choices about those goods to which we wish to devote our lives, we deceive ourselves if we think that the only limits to our choices are our imaginations. The Natural Law theorist John Finnis is right to point out that there are only a limited number of things which it makes sense to choose.[9] We need to abandon the idea of the neutral public square, and to think instead of the open public square, one in which people are free to choose between those reasonable life-plans which a society promotes.

We need a shared vision of the good life in our society which we can pursue in common, but it does not need to be an exhaustive one. It does not need to exclude the possibility of people choosing their own life-plans and it does not need to eliminate an area of personal responsibility for those choices in which people are not answerable to the community. As Amartya Sen has emphasised, there are good reasons for using law primarily as a tool to address manifest injustices, those things about which there is a widespread consensus that they are morally wrong, rather than in a vain attempt to build a perfectly just society.[10]

conclusion

Law needs a moral basis but this does not mean simply equating law with morality. What it does mean is that we need to restart a public debate about not just what is right but also about the common good for our society. It means disavowing the idea that law is merely a neutral umpire between differing individual conceptions of the good. It means affirming the idea that law should be the reflection of substantive, shared moral commitments, not merely a technical instrument for the promotion of particular interests within society.

references

1   What Bentham wrote, in *The Rationale of Reward* (London: Robert Heward, 1830), p. 206, was, "Prejudice apart, the game of push-pin is of equal value with the arts and sciences of music and poetry." In setting out his dispute with Bentham on this point, J.S. Mill misquoted Bentham as having written "Push-pin is as good as poetry": J.S. Mill, "Bentham," *Dissertations and Discussions*, Vol. I (London: Parker, 1859), p. 389.

2   John Rawls, *A Theory of Justice* (Belknap, 1971).

3   R. Dworkin, 'Liberalism', in S. Hampshire (ed.), *Public and Private Morality* (Cambridge: Cambridge University Press, 1978), p. 127.

4   John Finnis, 'On the Incoherence of Legal Positivism', *Notre Dame Law Review*, 75 (2000) p. 1598.

5   As long ago as 1897, Oliver Wendell Holmes Jr., legal sceptic and Justice of the US Supreme Court, said: "See how much more the world is governed today by Kant than by Bonaparte": O.W. Holmes, 'The Path of the Law', *Harvard Law Review*, 10 (1897) p. 478.

6   Brian Tamanaha, *Law as a Means to an End: Threat to the Rule of Law* (Cambridge: Cambridge University Press, 2006) p. 1.

7   Joseph Raz, *Ethics in the Public Domain: Essays in the Morality of Law and Politics* (Oxford: Clarendon Press, 1994), p. 324.

8   Michael Sandel, *Justice* (London: Allen Lane, 2009) p. 261.

9   John Finnis, *Natural Law and Natural Rights* (Oxford: Clarendon Press, 1981).

10 Amartya Sen, *The Idea of Justice* (London: Penguin, 2010).

Previous **Theos** reports:

Religion and Law

The proper relationship between religious commitment and the law of the land has always been contested and controversial. Nevertheless, the last 15 years have seen it become especially neuralgic in the UK, as ever more cases have found their way into the courts and the media.

Are human rights and religious commitment fully compatible? How far are minority legal orders permissible? Can freedom of conscience be reconciled with equality? What is the proper balance between Westminster and Strasbourg in such matters?

In this volume sixteen leading legal experts explore the relationship between religion and law in Britain today. None of the issues they examine is open to an easy or simple solution – and certainly not the old chestnut that "religion should be private". Each, however, is helped by application of intelligent and informed reflection, such as offered by the contributors.

Religion and Law offers some much needed light on an area all too often marked by its heat. It is invaluable reading for anyone who wishes to understand and contribute to one of the key debates of our time.

"Challenging, interesting and essential reading for anyone with an interest in the relationship between religion and the law. I don't agree with everything that is written but that is not necessary to still appreciate the sincerity and the quality of the arguments put forward. I recommend this book as offering insight and depth to anyone who is interested in this subject."

The Rt Hon Dominic Grieve QC MP, Attorney General

"A rare volume: a collection of essays, written mainly from a religious perspective, that avoids preachiness and proselytising. It provides a useful introduction to some of the areas in which religion sometimes rubs up against the law, offering not only food for thought but also guidance on what may or may not be legal."

Joshua Rozenberg, Legal Commentator

"This series of insightful essays from a broad range of experts both informs and illuminates this seemingly intractable topic, inevitably raising as many questions as it does answers."

Archbishop Peter Smith

£5

ISBN: 978-0-9562182-8-5

Theos